Personal Balanced Scorecard

The Way to Individual Happiness, Personal Integrity, and Organizational Effectiveness

Advance Praise for Personal Balanced Scorecard

Personal Balanced Scorecard offers individuals a sense of hope and a pathway to get there. Ultimately, all change is individual and personal and this book offers a practical guide for helping people turn personal missions into personal improvement actions. The frameworks and questions focus attention on the right issues in the right way.

—**Dave Ulrich,** author HR Value Proposition, partner The RBL Group, and Professor Ross School of Business, University of Michigan, USA

This book by Dr. Hubert Rampersad will help transform organizational leaders to the level they are probably unaware they can reach. Unlike so many other business books, this one presents a truly unique method that touches on every aspect of human nature: spiritual, physiological, mental, emotional, moral and ethical. All of these are integrated into the context of producing optimal organizational efficiency, through proper alignment of our personal ambition and objectives along with organizational vision and mission. This book provides truly unique set of tools and methodologies, which I wish I had the fortune of reading much sooner. The fundamentals rooted in Dr. Rampersad's PBSC model are timeless, and his highly practical tools presented in this book are designed for unpredictable and complex challenges of today and tomorrow.

—**Jeannette Lee,** Founder of Sytel, Inc., winner of the national Entrepreneurial Excellence Award in the field of Innovative Business Strategies category from the *Working Woman* magazine, and the Entrepreneurial Award by the Dialogue on Diversity. In 2001, White was listed as the *Washingtonian* Magazine's "100 Most Powerful Women in Washington."

Personal Balanced Scorecard offers a useful framework to help translate organizational strategies into personal development and improvement plans. By providing the tools to help turn strategy into action, this book can help any manager enhance his or her personal and professional success.

—**Mark Huselid,** Professor of HR Strategy, Rutgers University, USA, and co-author of the international bestsellers *The HR Scorecard* and *The Workforce Scorecard.*

Personal Balanced Scorecard is excellently on time and on target. It is one of the first tangible and useable means to provide for a person the opportunity to create, follow, measure and improve his own agenda. With PBSC, we start the long way towards a society in which the person will become the central focus point, with a responsibility that will be larger than ever before. In a world that will be more complex and tougher than seen and experienced so far. PBSC will make the current but more so the next generation better and stronger for the "personal age" that is about to arrive to all of us.

—**Professor Roel Pieper,** Chairman Favonius Ventures and former Vice President of Philips Electronics and Compaq Computer Corp.

Personal Balanced Scorecard provides a roadmap for the organizations of the future! Hubert Rampersad is one of the great thought leaders who are both helping organizations increase effectiveness and helping people have better lives. He is helping make the world a better place, and is one of the few consultants who look at the entire picture—not just a small part.

—**Marshall Goldsmith,** recognized by the American Management Association as one of the 50 great thinkers and leaders who have impacted the field of management over the past 80 years. He has appeared in: *The Wall Street Journal*—as one of the top ten executive educators, *Forbes*—as one of the five most-respected executive coaches and *The Economist*—as one of the most credible thought leaders in the new era of business.

Personal Balanced Scorecard is an outstanding contribution to the field of self- mastery and personal transformation. Written from a pragmatic viewpoint, this book is likely to help set your agenda for a radical shift from systems-driven change to selfled change. I often ask, if livelihood is for life, what is life for? Dr. Hubert Rampersad's work explores that question deeply and comes up with startling answers.

—Professor Debashis Chatterjee, Head, Centre for Leadership and Human Values, Indian Institute of Management, Lucknow, India and author of *Leading Consciously.*

In the world of organizational development and organizational change, many theorists have provided models and guidance on attempting to change the culture through leadership development and instilling a sense of personal responsibility in all employees. However, no theorist has provided an infrastructure such that the process that will change the culture is embedded in the organization. The Personal Balanced Scorecard process is integrally linked with organizational goals within individual performance plans for every employee to ensure change actually occurs and far richer outcomes are realized. It is critical in this time of globalization to take advantage of the intelligence of every employee and find ways of engaging them as a whole human being. We have used the PBSC ourselves and we have used it with clients and we've seen it work.

—Regina M. Bowden, Ph.D. and Eleanor Lester ABD,
Organizational Change Managers, Michigan

Personal Balanced Scorecard

The Way to Individual Happiness, Personal Integrity, and Organizational Effectiveness

by

Dr. Hubert K. Rampersad

Greenwich, Connecticut • www.infoagepub.com

Library of Congress Cataloging-in-Publication Data

Rampersad, Hubert K.
Personal balanced scorecard : the way to individual happiness, personal integrity, and organizational effectiveness / by Hubert Rampersad.
p. cm.
Includes bibliographical references and index.
ISBN-13: 978-1-59311-531-9 (pbk.)
ISBN-13: 978-1-59311-532-6 (hardcover)
1. Total quality management. 2. Self-actualization (Psychology) 3. Self-management (Psychology) 4. Performance–Measurement. 5. Organizational effectiveness I. Title.
HD62.15.R3596 2006
650.1–dc22

2006015684

ISBN-10:

Printed in the United States of America

To Rita, Rodney and Warren

no self-knowledge + no self-learning + no thinking + no doing + no challenge + no happiness + no alignment of personal ambition with personal behavior and shared ambition = no sustainable personal and organizational development
—Hubert Rampersad

CONTENTS

FOREWORD

This book by Dr. Hubert Rampersad will help transform organizational leaders to the level they are probably unaware they can reach. His Personal Balanced Scorecard (PBSC) concept integrates four main elements: internal, external, knowledge & learning, and financial. Unlike so many other business books, this one presents a truly unique method that touches on every aspect of human nature: spiritual, physiological, mental, emotional, moral and ethical. All of these are integrated into the context of producing optimal organizational efficiency, through proper alignment of our personal ambition and objectives along with organizational vision and mission.

I built my company successfully from scratch 19 years ago and sold it in January 2005. I cannot agree more with Dr. Rampersad with his PBSC concept. I feel it in my blood, sweat, and tears, all of the core elements discussed in this book and presented so methodically and logically. I transformed myself continually last two decades. I led an organization that was highly motivated and engaged, earning consistent respect and reputation from the industry. This required intense, self-disciplined, sharply focused training and continual development mentally, emotionally, spiritually, physically (especially during a three-year period in which I had to do a major business turnaround). This required good people and training all around, and equally importantly, it demanded extra-large sized heart, brain, and vision, with extra-small sized ego and wasteful, negative human emotion. I am not professing I reached all those levels, rather I am merely testifying that I endlessly strived to try to get there. This required total self-control. As Dr. Rampersad puts it, "you must first conquer yourself."

One of many valuable insights Dr. Rampersad presented in this book is the use of left- and right- sides of the brain. I have found so many highly-

Personal Balanced Scorecard, pages xi–xii

trained company managers perform "just enough" to reach the level of success that they are content with, and meanwhile many of them do not begin to know or recognize what they don't know. They are developed to be strong in logic, methods, systems and processes, yet they are less developed to be strong in intuition, instinct, vision and creativity. They use left side of their brain more than their right side. I have also met so many successful entrepreneurs who have strong and proven intuition, yet they are weak in building logical, methodical, and repeatable organizational blocks in order to successfully scale.

This leads to missed opportunities for continual self-growth, both individually and organizationally. In a highly dynamic, competitive global marketplace in which we are often caught surprised by the next form and type of competitive threat, it has now become our social responsibility to continually improve, transform, and contribute. Short term, we must make continual improvements; and long term, we must lead to or effectuate breakthrough-level results.

This book provides truly unique set of tools and methodologies, which I wish I had the fortune of reading much sooner. The fundamentals rooted in Dr. Rampersad's PBSC model are timeless, and his highly practical tools presented in this book are designed for unpredictable and complex challenges of today and tomorrow.

—Jeannette Lee
Founder of Sytel, Inc.
May 2006

PREFACE

Science is organized knowledge. Wisdom is organized life.

—Immanuel Kant (1724–1804)

The Personal Balanced Scorecard (PBSC) is a journey into the inner self, where values, hopes, dreams and aspirations lie quietly waiting to be discovered. Taking the journey as an individual allows you to view your life objectively and authentically as a whole person and provides a roadmap of your dreams and aspirations translated into manageable and measurable milestones.

As a part of the Total Performance Scorecard (TPS) process which I introduced in 2003 in *Total Performance Scorecard: Redefining Management to Achieve Performance with Integrity,* and which has been translated into more than 20 languages, the Personal Balanced Scorecard can also be an effective way for managers to coach others to achieve integrity and alignment between work and life. The benefit comes from changing individual behavior in order to drive organizational effectiveness, enhance performance, and increase self-awareness, personal responsibility and motivation. PBSC is an integral part of this organic and holistic Total Performance Scorecard process, which is an organizational and cultural change tool and a method for ongoing effectiveness. Its uniqueness lies in aligning and combination Personal and Organizational goals to result in Individual Performance Plans for each employee. The focus of this book is the PBSC portion, which comprises a search for self-knowledge, self-discovery and self-mastery.

The starting point in this new concept is gaining an insight into oneself. This allows people to manage their emotional and spiritual intelligence, and expand their horizons. It helps them understand and master themselves, and thus gain a deeper commitment to self-responsibility. After all,

Personal Balanced Scorecard, pages xiii–xvi

personal development is a person's own responsibility. It is one's ethical duty and responsibility to develop oneself and become more proactive—for one's own good, and for that of loved ones, work, organization, country, and the world of which one is a part. Personal coaching using the PBSC method is an inner, spiritual and ethical learning process, if one is open to it. It has to do with the balance of one's IQ, emotional intelligence and spiritual intelligence; a balance between the left and right side of the brain.

Using the PBSC method, it's easy to effectively manage and coach yourself. It's equally effective to have a trusted friend, spouse or colleague help coach you. If you choose to work with a trusted friend, it's important that you feel safe in being your true and authentic self in the presence of this friend. The journey inside oneself is sacred and should be treated in a special way.

Implementation of one's PBSC leads to a richer and more fulfilling way of life. It leads to continuous development and use of one's talents, self-learning, greater awareness of one's responsibilities and self-discipline, development of one's creativity and ethical behavior. Through this, one creates the conditions for continuous and gradual development of oneself so that it becomes routine to enjoy improving every day, and to do good things right the first time.

PBSC offers a systematic and integrated approach to the transformation of people in organizations, and to impact strategy, culture and organizational effectiveness. This system and the ongoing improvement Plan-Do-Act-Challenge (PDAC) cycle are based on several new models, guidelines and tools that have been proven in practice. A way of life in conformity with the PBSC and the PDAC cycle results in *flow*, which is the process of total involvement in life, whereby you feel happy with your challenging activities, enjoy your work more thoroughly and spend your spare time more effectively.

What I have in mind with the introduction of PBSC in organizations, is to narrow the huge gap that exists between the way people deal with their colleagues and the way they deal with their friends and family. In recent years, I have applied the PBSC system in large companies in many countries, and have observed that implementing the PBSC method results in a step-by-step increase in individual happiness, consciousness, self-learning and creativity, at work as well as in life in general. It is a process of breaking habits, letting go, and dealing more effectively by using both your logic and your intuition. It is also a development and learning process, which transforms people into happy, inwardly involved, and committed employees. This will not only allow them to contribute exceptionally but will also persuade them to support, defend, promote and love their organization.

This approach differs fundamentally from traditional personal coaching and scorecards methods. PBSC brings an inspirational and spiritual learning process that measurably, concretely and routinely improves personal effectiveness, thus reinforcing the work/life balance and the honesty and trustworthiness of the organization. An integrated breathing and silence exercise is introduced and encouraged which imparts life energy to the body. In time, this helps transform personal ambition into purposeful action. Ambition without the energy to proceed to action is senseless.

The emphasis here lies with intrinsic motivation, which is inherently pleasurable, while extrinsic motivation is not. Intrinsic motivation is that which arises from within—doing something because you enjoy it—while extrinsic motivation means people are seeking a reward, such as money. Money has lost its impact on employees' motivation. People are happiest when they are given freedom, challenges, and control over their lives. This requires the opportunity to build self-respect, trust, self-responsibility, and inner involvement. The PBSC method has a *"drive out fear"* philosophy, which creates the conditions that eliminate employees' fears, and enables them to realize their full potential and contribute creatively. With no fear, less management intervention, and higher autonomy and well-being, work becomes more satisfying.

Improving organizational performance requires a highly engaged and happy workforce. In this book, I also introduce a method to align individuals' personal ambitions with the organizational shared ambition, which is a prerequisite for employee engaged and a happy workforce. Alignment means linking the organization's mission, vision, and core values with the individual's personal mission, vision, and key roles. This lies at the heart of successful organizational and cultural change. After all, it is difficult to change the organization, but if we change ourselves, the organization will change with us. This personal change involves individual learning and unlearning based on the PBSC system. This self-learning must be converted into collective learning, which leads ultimately to sustainable organizational change.

Traditional balanced scorecard and organizational change implementations tend to be insufficiently committed to learning, and rarely take personal behavioral change into account. That's why numerous case studies indicate that the implementation of the balanced scorecard according to Kaplan & Norton have been disappointing at best in North America, and in Europe and South America even more so. Bringing people involvement into balanced scorecards according to the PBSC method is a step-by-step, holistic process that not only involves individual buy-in but also stimulates individual and team learning in order to realize sustainable performance improvement.

PBSC also differs in essential ways from Stephen Covey's brilliant *7/8 Habits of Highly Effective People*. It picks up where Stephen Covey left off. Specifically, the measurable translation of personal vision into concrete personal targets and improvement actions is missing in his '7/8 Habits' concept. His concept doesn't provide an organizational process and concrete reference framework that allows this translation to routinely happen inside companies. The PBSC has a holistic structure that can be adopted and integrated with the current organizational goals and objectives or with the current Organizational Balanced Scorecard. In addition, the PBSC integrates the individual's aspirations with a collective ambition, balancing the personal with the organizational shared ambition, embedding ethical behavior in the individual's mind. It also links individual capabilities with collective talent management, helping to provide a strong, sustainable future. These are not provided in Covey's concept. The consequences of this are sub-optimization and personal improvements that will only work superficially and temporarily.

PBSC is, in contrast with Stephen Covey's system, a continuous discovery of personal integrity, self-mastery, and happiness at work as well as in private life, amalgamating both into one complete, integrated and fulfilled life. Despite the above comments, the '7/8 Habits' is a splendid concept that makes a most useful contribution to the formulation and implementation of PBSC. The introduction of PBSC is almost like launching an integrated 9th habit that has been proven in practice to produce better and sustainable results. The general, practical and simple nature of the PBSC method makes this book suitable for anyone who wants to develop himself on a routine and lasting basis. It's a synergistic product of the minds and efforts of many business writers and thinkers, from whom I have benefited. I am grateful for their inspiration: they deserve much of the credit.

I would also like to express my thanks to Ada Wynston, Eleanor Lester, and Dr. Regina Bowden for their contributions to the realization of this book. I am very grateful to Robert Angel, Robert Bense, and Fred Engel who have given constructive feedback and encouragement. Thanks are also due to Jeannett Lee (founder of Sytel, Inc.) for writing the foreword of this book and for her important suggestions.

Writing this book has been a challenge to me, as well as a learning process. A special word of thanks to my wife Rita and my sons Rodney and Warren, who inspired and stimulated me to take this challenge and to enjoy. I wish you lots of success on the road to a happier and more successful life, and on your voyage towards enhancing personal and company value. Feedback is welcome at *h.rampersad@tps-international.com* or *info@total-performance-scorecard.com* and *www.Total-Performance-Scorecard.com*

—Hubert Rampersad
President and Chairman of the Board of Directors
TPS International Inc., California

CHAPTER 1

INTRODUCTION

Business is more about emotions than most businesspeople care to admit.

—Daniel Kahneman, Professor of psychology and public affairs at Princeton University and winner of the 2002 Nobel Prize in economics

Lack of engagement is endemic, and is causing large and small organizations all over the world to incur excess costs, under perform on critical tasks, and create widespread customer dissatisfaction. The annual financial loss in the US due to disengagement of managers and employees is about $300B US (Gallup Poll, 2005). Improving organizational performance requires a highly engaged and happy workforce. Research on happiness in the workplace suggests that worker well-being plays a major role in organizational performance and that there is a strong relationship between worker happiness and workplace engagement. The *Gallup Management Journal* (Jerry Krueger and Emily Killham, 2005) surveyed U.S. employees to probe their perceptions of how happiness and well-being affect their job performance. Gallup researchers examined employee responses to see which factors differed most strongly among engaged employees and those who were not engaged or actively disengaged (See boxed text below).

Personal Balanced Scorecard, pages 1–17

At Work, Feeling Good Matters

Happy employees are better equipped to handle workplace relationships, stress, and change, according to the latest* GMJ *survey

The *Gallup Management Journal* surveyed U.S. employees to probe their perceptions of how happiness and well-being affect their job performance. Gallup researchers examined employee responses to see which factors differed most strongly among engaged employees (27% of respondents) and those who were not engaged (59%) or actively disengaged (14%). This research shows that supervisors play a crucial role in worker well-being and engagement. The sidebar below show "The Three Types of Employees" and the results from the survey in which respondents were asked to respond to the statement "My supervisor focuses on my strengths or positive characteristics"; 77% of engaged workers strongly agreed with the statement. Just 23% of not-engaged and 4% of actively disengaged workers strongly agreed that their supervisor focused on their strengths or positive characteristics. When survey respondents were asked how they would characterize their interactions with their co-workers, 86% of engaged employees said their interactions with co-workers were always positive or mostly positive. The findings for less engaged workers showed significantly different results: 72% of not-engaged workers characterized these interactions as always or mostly positive, compared to just 45% of actively disengaged workers. These findings indicate that a positive relationship with the supervisor has an important effect on engagement. They suggest that people with higher levels of job engagement enjoy substantially more positive interactions with their co-workers than do their less engaged counterparts.

The Three Types of Employees

1. ENGAGED employees work with passion and feel a profound connection to their company. They drive innovation and move the organization forward.
2. NOT-ENGAGED employees are essentially "checked out." They're sleepwalking through their workday, putting time—but not energy or passion—into their work.
3. ACTIVELY DISENGAGED employees aren't just unhappy at work; they're busy acting out their unhappiness. Every day, these workers undermine what their engaged coworkers accomplish.

When American employees were asked how often they feel challenged at work, 61% of engaged workers said they feel challenged very often. In contrast, just 49% of not-engaged and 24% of actively disengaged workers indicated that they very often feel challenged at work. It appears that while most American workers do perceive their jobs as being at least somewhat challenging, engaged employees lead the way in this respect. The respondents were also asked how often they feel frustrated at work. 39% of engaged employees indicated that they rarely or never feel frustrated at work. In contrast, 60% actively

Supervisors Are Crucial to Worker Engagement

When respondents were asked to respond to the statement "My supervisor focuses on my strengths or positive characteristics," 77% of engaged workers strongly agreed with the statement, compared to just 23% of not-engaged and 4% of actively disengaged workers.

Percentage of employees who strongly agreed that *"My supervisor focuses on my strengths or positive characteristcs"*

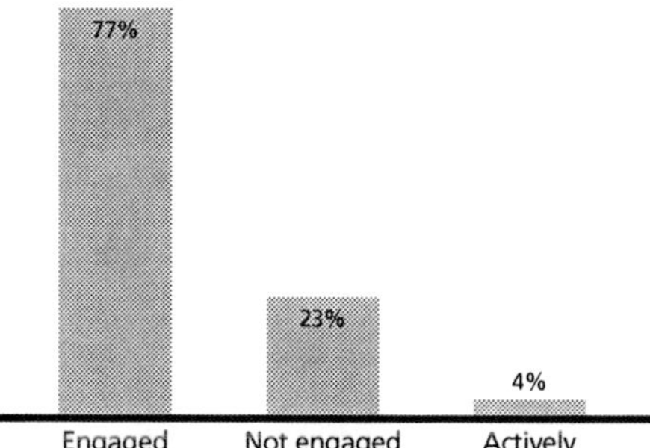

Source: Gallup Organization   Graphic by Tommy McCall

disengaged workers and 26% of not-engaged employees said they very often feel frustrated. These responses suggest that while engaged workers *do* feel challenged at work, they view these challenges in a much more positive light than do less engaged workers. The *GMJ* also wanted to find out if workers' feelings of self-worth had an effect on their engagement. They do. When asked how difficult it would be for their employer to replace them, 54% of disengaged employees said it would be extremely or somewhat difficult for their employer to replace them, compared to 76% of engaged employees. Engaged workers also felt significantly more secure at their workplaces: 54% of engaged workers felt more secure at work than they did a year ago, but only 36% of not-engaged workers and just 18% of actively disengaged workers agreed that they felt more secure at work than they did a year ago. To probe the connection between happiness at work and happiness outside the office, the survey asked respondents how much happiness they experience at work. 86% of engaged workers said they very often felt happy while at work. Only 11% of actively disengaged and 48% of not engaged employees stated that they, too, were very often happy at work. In response to the question "How much of the happiness you experience overall would you say comes from your work life? 45% of engaged employees said they get a great deal of their overall happiness from their work life, compared to just 19% of not-engaged and 8% of actively disengaged employees.

These findings suggest that while most workers experience varying degrees of happiness and well-being at work, engaged workers get the most from these feelings. They reported higher levels of overall life satisfaction. Negative feelings at work also seem to spill over into actively disengaged workers' home lives. The survey asked respondents if they had three or more days in the past month when work stress caused them to behave poorly with friends or family members. More than half (54%) of actively disengaged workers and 31% of not-engaged workers answered yes to this question, while just 17% of engaged workers answered yes.

The results of the *GMJ* Employee Engagement Index survey also show a strong relationship between worker happiness and workplace engagement. Happy and engaged employees are much more likely to have a positive relationship with their boss, are better equipped to handle new challenges and changes, feel they are more valued by their employers, handle stress more effectively, and are much more satisfied with their lives. The graphic below illustrates the cost of disengagement.

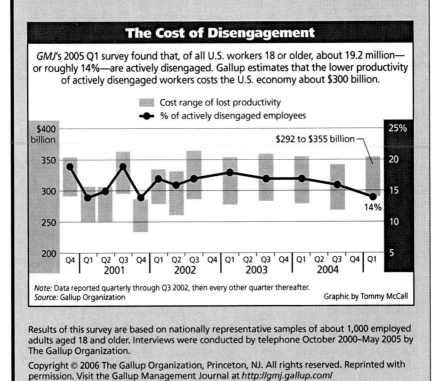

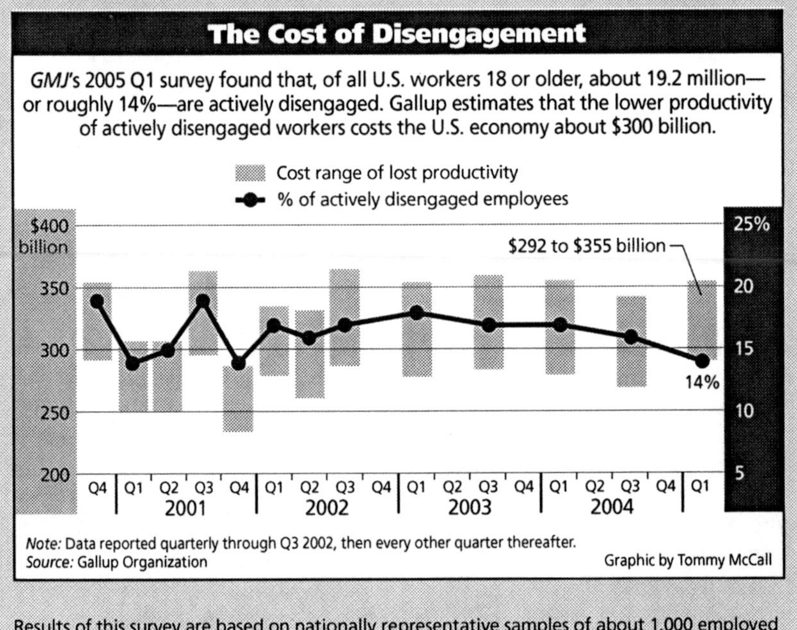
The Cost of Disengagement
GMJ's 2005 Q1 survey found that, of all U.S. workers 18 or older, about 19.2 million—or roughly 14%—are actively disengaged. Gallup estimates that the lower productivity of actively disengaged workers costs the U.S. economy about $300 billion.
Cost range of lost productivity
% of actively disengaged employees
$400 billion
350
300
250
200
25%
20
15
10
5
$292 to $355 billion
14%
Q4 Q1 Q2 Q3 Q4 Q1 Q2 Q3 Q4 Q1 Q2 Q3 Q4 Q1 Q2 Q3 Q4 Q1
2001
2002
2003
2004
Note: Data reported quarterly through Q3 2002, then every other quarter thereafter.
Source: Gallup Organization
Graphic by Tommy McCall

Results of this survey are based on nationally representative samples of about 1,000 employed adults aged 18 and older. Interviews were conducted by telephone October 2000–May 2005 by The Gallup Organization.

Other research shows that when employees have tense or strained relationships with their manager or colleagues, this may increase the level of stress (Anna Diamantopoulou, 2002). The boxed text below shows the impact of stress at work in the European Union.

Stress Costs the European Union US$ 26 Billion Annually

Illness as a result of stress at work costs the European Union US$ 26 billion per year. Over 41 million people have been unable to work for a short or a longer period of time because of stress, the second most frequent work-related illness. The above amount includes the cost of absence of employees and health-care cost, not the related labor productivity losses. It is estimated that this overload at work leads to one-fifth of all heart diseases in the Union. It stimulates smoking, bad diets and use of alcohol and as such also contributes to the development of cancer. Muscles and skeleton (especially neck, arms and lower back) are affected. In the psychological domain, fears, depressions and suicides are mentioned as a result of stress, resulting from a lack of input over own work conditions, monotony at work, hectic deadlines and bullying supervisors. Possible solutions could be changing the organizational culture, increased worker participation in decision-making, open communication, clarity about the position of each employee and coaching/training. Women suffer slightly more from stress than men. The problems are present on all levels, in every role and in every sector. In the United States, 11 million people suffer from stress, in terms of percentage, around half the European Union numbers. In the United States, it causes over half of all absences.

Source: Anna Diamantopoulou, European Commissioner of Social Affairs and Employment, Brussels, 2002

The International Labour Organization (ILO) defines organizational stress as *"Harmful physical and emotional responses that occur when the job requirements do not match the capabilities, resources or needs of the workers."* Burnout is a physical, mental, and emotional response to constant levels of high stress. It produces feelings of hopelessness, powerlessness, cynicism, resentment and failure—as well as stagnation and reduced labour productivity. Research shows that when employees have tense or strained relationships with their manager or colleagues, this could increase their levels of stress. In a survey conducted by the American Psychological Association in 2004, nearly two-thirds of all respondents indicated that their work lives had a significant impact on their stress levels, while one in four had called in sick as a result of stress at work. Organizations that understand the connections between worker stress and health and wellbeing can help their employees manage stress and find balance in their work and personal lives. When they do, productivity and engagement improve (*Gallup Management Journal,* 2005).

According to the National Institute for Occupational Safety and Health (1983):

- Stress is linked to physical and mental health, and decreased willingness to take on new and creative endeavors
- Job burnout is experienced by 25% to 40% of U.S. workers
- Stress has a major negative impact on productivity.
- Depression, only one type of stress reaction, is responsible for more days lost than any other single factor
- $300 billion, or $7,500.00 per employee, is spent annually in the U.S. on stress related compensation claims, reduced productivity, absenteeism, health insurance claims, and direct medical expenses (nearly 50% higher for workers who report stress symptoms)

A Gallop Poll (2000) reported:

- 80% of workers feel stress on the job; nearly half say they need help in learning how to manage stress and 42% say their coworkers need such help
- 14% of respondents had felt like striking a coworker in the past year, but didn't
- 25% have felt like screaming or shouting because of job stress; 10% are concerned about an individual at work they fear could become violent
- 9% are aware of an assault or violent act in their workplace and 18% had experienced some sort of threat or verbal intimidation in the past year

According to Regina Bowden (2006), 60% to 90% of all doctor visits in the U.S. are stress-related. The leading six causes of death in the U.S. are all stress-related: heart disease, cancer, lung disease, accidents, cirrhosis of the liver, suicide. Her research shows that the emotional and physical impact of stress are: immune response and deficiency, increased aggression, memory loss, cognitive impairment, obesity, difficulty responding to challenges, chronic ailments, narrow-mindedness, aging, foggy thinking, sleep disruptions, diminished productivity, mental absence, depression, and rage. And that the biggest stressors in US-organizations are related to the feeling as though you: have no control over your future, aren't valued for your efforts, are in the "out" group rather than the "in" group, are not "heard," get "mixed messages" about goals, don't get relevant feedback, and work harder/longer than your rewards warrant. Research done by HeartMath Research Center in California shows how stress and emotions impact learning and performance (Rollin McCraty, 2002).

This book entails some new and unique principles that will help organizations tread the above mentioned problems and the demanding and often frustrating road towards sustained employee engagement improvement and stress reduction. In order to realize this, executives should recognize that their organization's people are the most critical factor in their company's ability to perform better. They have to realize that people—not cost cutting or innovative products—make the difference between high performers and market laggards in the years ahead. According to the most recent High Performance Workforce Study conducted by Accenture in North America, financial services executives unanimously agreed that the performance of their workforces could be substantially improved. For instance, only 11 percent of these executives believed the overall skill level of their workforce to be 'industry leading'. Employee engagement and retention, in particular, are major problems faced by many financial services companies. Accenture discovered that HR and learning programs in most organizations do not deliver the kind of results that executives hope for and; no more than 27 percent of financial services executives said they were very satisfied with the progress on their most important HR and learning initiatives. For some initiatives, the percentage was as low as zero (improving worker productivity) or 2 percent (improving employee engagement).

Many naive managers still believe salary to be the most important motivator. They still do not realize that offering new challenges, showing one's commitment and honesty, being open to feedback, and giving autonomy and support are the main motivators. They are not aware that organizations are living systems—where people live—and that employees need to be treated as human beings. It is time that executives and managers realize that their thinking and actions need to change. That what is required is an attitude stimulating workplace engagement, learning, and enjoyment, and a smarter work environment that is free from fear. It is also time for managers and human resource officers to realize that the solution to many problems lies in employee work/life balance, as well as linking personal ambition with the organization's ambition. According to Charles Handy:

> The companies that survive longest are the ones that work out what they uniquely can give to the world not just through growth or money but their excellence, their respect for others, or their ability to make people happy. Some call those things a soul.

Bill George, former Chairman of Medtronic Inc. said:

> In the 21st Century great companies will figure out how to tap into people's hearts—their passion and their desires to make a difference through their work. Those companies that link these passions to the generation of innovative ideas will have the capacity to sustain their growth for decades.

In this book, I shall focus on the new tasks of managers to continuously improve the quality of life of their staff, not only at the workplace, but also in their spare time on the basis of the methods and techniques presented here. Following such practices would encourage employees to continuously feel free and safe, and able to accept bigger challenges, and through this, provide enjoyment in work and experience well-being and happiness. This attitude will also have its effect on customers and shareholders, improving their quality of life and adding to their well-being and satisfaction. It is therefore critical that managers realize that their employees' home situation (healthy or not) has an impact on their work performance. This can no longer be ignored. Managers have to look beyond their own noses, and understand that those who are not able to function well in their families cannot function well at work either. Managers need to rapidly unlearn the practice of ignoring the private circumstances of employees. The Personal Balanced Scorecard is a new management concept that can help solve the problems that I have been talking about. It has been proven in practice since the time it was launched in 2003 as part of my Total Performance Scorecard book (Rampersad, 2003). The boxed text that follows shows some praises for this book.

Praise for Total Performance Scorecard™

"Hubert Rampersad takes the balanced scorecard and other management ideas and puts them in a framework of personal integrity. By unifying organizational change strategies with individual ethics he has written an outstanding synthesis, which is addressed to the corporate challenges of managing in the 21st century."

—Paul Bracken
Professor of Management, Yale School of Management

"Dr. Rampersad's latest book makes a most useful contribution to the neverending challenge of aligning individual motivations and behaviors with enterprise performance aspirations."

—Jon R. Katzenbach
co-author of the international bestseller *The Wisdom of Teams* and editor of *The Work of Teams*, a Harvard Business Review compendium

"This book should be read by anyone interested in affecting organizational improvement and change. By expanding and integrating concepts such as the Balanced Scorecard, Total Quality Management, Performance Management and Competence Management into one overall framework, which he calls the Total Performance Scorecard, Dr. Rampersad gives us a new blueprint for creating a learning organization in which personal and organizational performance and learning mutually reinforce each other."

—Cornelis A. de Kluyver
Henry Y. Hwang Dean and Professor of Management, Peter F. Drucker Graduate School of Management, Claremont Graduate University.

"Hubert Rampersad has amassed and synthesized a huge amount of material . . . The book serves as a practical guide, in that there are numerous exercises and business illustrations."

—From the Foreword by Dorothy A. Leonard
The William J. Abernathy Professor of Business Administration
Harvard Business School

"Hubert Rampersad's *Total Performance Scorecard* is management technology for the enlightened age. Rampersad beautifully explains how anyone can apply principles of motivational alignment and individualistic scorecard techniques to engineer an organization for continuous learning."

—Dr. James O'Toole
Massachusetts Institute of Technology

"*Total Performance Scorecard* is a thorough, systematic, and integrated approach to individual and organization success. It synthesizes and extends personal, leadership, and organization theories of change and success. It offers managers tools to do a complete physical for their organization and it offers individuals an encyclopedia of knowledge about personal success."

—Dave Ulrich
Professor of Business, University of Michigan

"For organizational leaders looking to achieve outstanding results through the Balanced Scorecard, this book by Dr. Hubert Rampersad is essential reading. Through his exceptional framework of the Total Performance Scorecard (TPS), Dr. Rampersad takes the ideas of the Balanced Scorecard to even greater heights. His system creates a completely new vision for bringing individual, team and organizational performance to higher levels, through a comprehensive set of tools that can easily be applied to a broad range of organizational systems. The TPS goes beyond individual behavior to the more challenging goal of measuring and then changing organizational processes that limit and even impede individual performance. In this sense, it goes to the heart of a learning organization in which measuring systems facilitate the personal development of employees. Peter Senge broke the mindset barrier and showed how systems thinking and system change are essential to support individual development. The strength of TPS, however, is that it measures personal development in the context of organizational development. This highly interactive process creates the foundation for dynamic change where everyone can benefit from constant learning and improvement. Dr. Rampersad's brilliance lies in bringing Peter Senge's ideas of system symbiosis into alignment with ideas of personal ambition, vision and mission. When leaders can accurately measure true performance—low, average or outstanding—it is possible for the ideal to become a reality.

—George A. Kohlrieser
Professor of Leadership & Organizational Behavior IMD, Switzerland

I am amazed with the fact that the *Total Performance Scorecard (TPS)* concept is spreading like gospel. Dr. Hubert Rampersad's innovative and pragmatic approach to combine organizational and personal performance agendas into one line of thinking helps organizational participants to come up with tangible solutions to current performance and leadership issues.

—Padmakumar Nair, Ph.D., D.Sc., MBA
Organization, Strategy and International Management
School of Management, University of Texas–Dallas

"There is often a disconnect between organizational goal-setting and the way individuals establish individual objectives and are reviewed. *Total Performance Scorecard* fills the gap with a complete system that unites individual and organizational performance scorecards, linking continuous improvement efforts with individual learning and development programs. If you are looking for a comprehensive toolkit for improving results in your company, this is the book to buy."

—Philip Anderson
Professor of Entrepreneurship
INSEAD Alumni Fund Chair in Entrepreneurship, Director, 3i Venturelab

"The United States Air Force is trying to become more accountable for performance using the Balanced Scorecard method, but I like the way Dr. Hubert Rampersad has tied the BSC to a Personal Balanced Scorecard. It's almost like Kaplan & Norton meet Stephen Covey"

—Bob Marx
United States Air Force

"Successful companies are High Performance Systems, something that is true today even more than ever. A condition to make these levels of High Performance possible is the alignment of personal and organizational targets and interests, irrespective of company levels or sectors. The Total Performance Scorecard (TPS) is a new management instrument that introduces this alignment and creates value based, ethical acting on a sustainable foundation. Dr. Hubert Rampersad has achieved a large and very important jump forward with the presentation of this concept."

—Professor Dr. Kuno Rechkemmer
Director DaimlerChrysler, Germany

Total Performance Scorecard (TPS) encompasses an amalgamation and expansion of the concepts of Personal Balanced Scorecard (PBSC), Organizational Balanced Scorecard (OBSC), Talent Management (TM) and Total Quality Management (TQM). It is defined as a systematic process of continuous, gradual, and routine improvement, development, and learning that is focused on a sustainable increase of personal and organizational

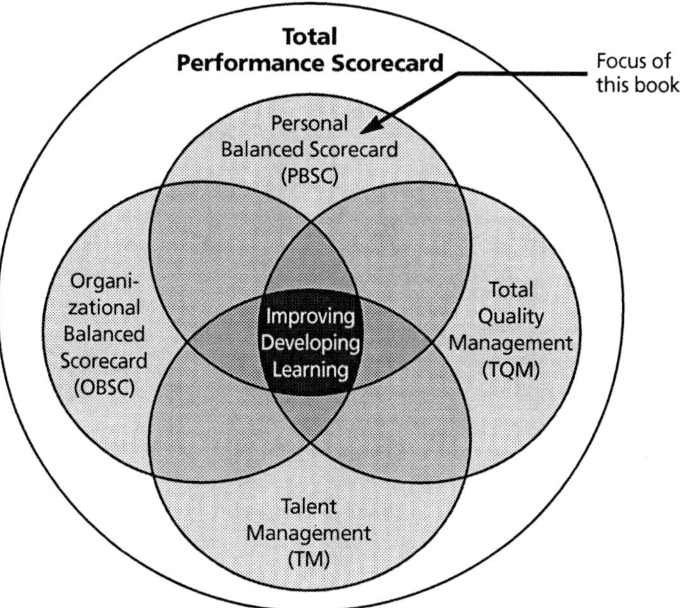

Figure 1.1. The Interrelated Modules of the TPS Concept

performances. Improving, developing, and learning are the three fundamental powers in this holistic management concept. They are closely interrelated and must be kept in balance. Figure 1.1 illustrates the correlation between the modules of the Total Performance Scorecard. This philosophy includes a synthesis of the four closely related management concepts to form a harmonious whole. There are overlaps between these concepts, as may be seen in the figure. The shaded area in the center illustrates the similarities between these four management concepts. Improving, developing, and learning together represent much of this common area. This book focuses mainly on the PBSC module, including the links to the OBSC, TM, and TQM modules. Specific areas of focus are: personal/leadership development, performance coaching, change management, organizational learning, working smarter, teamwork, reducing stress and burnout, and managing diversity. The learning goals of this book are described in the following box.

Learning Objectives

After reading this book and applying its concepts, as an *individual* you,

- will be able to tackle stress
- will be able to understand and manage yourself better

- will be able to increase your self-awareness, self-regulation and empathy
- will be able to enjoy your work much more, spend your free time much better, and create healthier relationships with your family members
- will discover your unconscious motives, deal better with inner conflicts, create positive energy, act more proactively, and strengthen your sense of self-responsibility
- will be able to increase personal integrity and act according to your conscience
- will be able to organize your time effectively
- will be able, on the basis of the Plan-Do-Act-Challenge cycle, to seek out new challenges and develop related skills
- can increase your personal effectiveness
- can develop a way of life which will result in a gradual increase in happiness, consciousness, pleasure, passion, self-learning and creativity, at work as well as in your free time

As a *manager*, you

- will be able to tackle lack of employee engagement
- will be able to develop a workforce of committed employees, which will not only contribute exceptionally to the organization, but also support, defend, promote and love it
- will be able to reinforce honesty and trustworthiness in yourself and the organization
- will know how to create a climate of trust within the organization and eliminate fear and distrust
- will be able to create conditions for a real learning organization
- will know, how to routinely bring about the maximum personal development of employees and to manage, develop and utilize their talents effectively
- will know how to bring about the best fit between employee and create lasting conditions for more self-guidance, inner involvement and reduction of stress and burnout for your employees
- will know how to set up an effective appraisal system, with a direct link to the balanced scorecard of the employees as well as of the organization
- will improve the ability of people to work productively and harmoniously together as a team and create quality results

The benefits of the PBSC system include—

For the individual:

- Greater individual understanding of the self and increased self-esteem
- Self-actualization

- Greater enjoyment and inner involvement with the work
- Working smarter instead of harder
- Higher usage of individual's mental capacity and productivity
- Increased personal responsibility

For the manager:

- Higher employee engagement
- Higher customer satisfaction
- Improved employee performance
- Iintrinsically motivated employees
- Less absenteeism, turnover, and grievances for the organization
- Individual and team empowerment
- Increased innovation
- Effective diversity management
- And ultimately, sustainable organizational effectiveness

The Personal Balanced Scorecard differs in essential ways from Stephen Covey's brilliant *7/8 Habits of Highly Effective People*. The boxed text given shows the difference between these two concepts.

Personal Balanced Scorecard versus Stephen Covey's *7/8 Habits of Highly Effective People*

Stephen Covey's *7 Habits of Highly Effective People* is about personal leadership with fairness, integrity, honesty and human dignity as the key words. His new book, The *8th Habit* adds that every individual has within himself the means for perfection, if only they can manage to balance the four human attributes: talent, need, conscience and passion. According to Stephen Covey, we face in today's era of the eighth habit, a more complex and challenging world than in the last decade (era of the seven habits). Independence, individualism and autonomy are constantly increasing in all facets of our lives. According to him, this implies the need to manage oneself more and more and not rely on others. Covey's approach is focused on personal leadership without any concrete and measurable reference framework. The Personal Balanced Scorecard (PBSC) picks up where Stephen Covey leaves off. Specifically, the PBSC translates the personal vision into concrete personal targets and actions for improvement, providing the basis for balancing personal aspirations with personal behavior.

Additionally, the PBSC is the foundation for linking the individual with the organization. Through the PBSC the individual's aspirations are integrated with a collective ambition, embedding ethical behavior and holistically linking capabilities with collective talent management. The consequences of neglecting any of these are personal and organizational sub-optimization with only temporary improvement. Without a holistic approach, the personal foundation will not be stable or sustainable enough to support the acceptance of new challenges and the development of skills related to these challenges. Pleasure at work, more effective use of free time and a good work/life balance are compromised. The PBSC is a continuing journey of discovery towards perfection, personal integrity, self-mastery, engagement, and happiness, at work as well as in people's personal lives, so as to amalgamate both lives into one fulfilling and integrated whole. Despite the above criticism the 7/8 habits is a splendid concept that makes a most useful contribution to the formulation and implementation of a PBSC. The introduction of the PBSC is almost like launching an integrated ninth habit that has been proven in practice to produce better and sustainable results, not only for the individual but also for the collective or organization.

This book consists of two parts. Part I has to do with the PBSC as an instrument for individual development, personal effectiveness, and growth in life. The emphasis is on excelling in everything that you do and choice in developing your future. This part is for everyone who wants a happier, more fulfilling life. You may be facing new life challenges. You may be at a crossroads in your career and don't know how to go on. You may be unemployed. You may be a mother, a college student, a factory worker, a call centre handler, and a retail clerk. This book provides you a unique instrument which when applied will give you new energy and enthusiasm for new challenges. Part I is usefule for individuals, personal coaches, career advisors, outplacement offices, job re-integration offices and recruitment and selection agencies. Part II describes the PBSC as an instrument to increase employee well-being and engagement at work and enhance the employee's unique talents. It has to do with having fun in the workplace, increasing labor productivity, lowering sick leave, and increasing work enjoyment in order to gain competitive advantages for the organization. It is possible to use Part I separately from Part II.

Part I beginning with Chapter 2 describes the essence of the Personal Balance Scorecard. Personal ambition, critical success factors, objectives, performance measures, targets and improvement actions are described in this chapter and illustrated with practical cases. Personal ambition to me denotes the combination of personal mission, vision, and key roles. An integral breathing and silence exercise is introduced, which will assist you in formulating and implementing your personal ambition effectively and allow deep self-reflection in assessing personal alignment and happiness continuously. This activity will train and exercise your brain, help you to pay attention to your inner voice and help you to achieve control over your consciousness. From this exercise, you will get energy to turn your ambition into action. This chapter also discusses the cause and effect chain, in which the connections between the various personal goals in the PBSC are visualized. This is important, because all goals should be related and have an effect on each other. Furthermore, a method is introduced to award priorities to the personal improvement actions.

Chapter 3 describes the implementation of the PBSC according to the unique Plan-Do-Act-Challenge (PDAC) cycle. This results in a step-by-step increase in happiness, awareness, enjoyment, learning and creativity at work and beyond. The implementation of your PBSC according to the PDAC cycle can lead to total involvement in life. It contributes to creating and sustaining a flow experience where you are so involved and happy with a new challenge that you forget everything around you.

In Chapter 4, I discuss more closely, the balance between personal ambition and personal behavior. It is necessary to bring both these elements in line to develop inner peace, personal charisma, and authenticity, and to improve personal integrity, trustworthiness and ethical behavior. In this chapter I also introduce a formula for self-knowledge. I also elaborate on the importance of balance between personal ambition and shared ambition stimulating commitment, trust, inner involvement and motivation of the employees. After all, an organization is a living organism because of its people. Employees must be treated as people.

Part II beginning with Chapter 5 is totally dedicated to the balance between these two ambitions. It has to do with reaching a high degree of compatibility between personal and organization goals, and mutual value adding. As an extension of this, I will also discuss the Organizational Balance Scorecard (OBSC). The OBSC encompasses the organizational mission, vision, core values, critical success factors, objectives, performance measures, targets, and improvement actions, which are divided into four different perspectives. I call the organizational mission, vision, and core values together the shared ambition. To realize the "best fit" between employee and organization, I introduce in this concept an ambition meeting between manager and employee. The ambition meeting is an informal, voluntary, and intimate conversation between both parties that takes place periodically with the ambition of that employee and the shared ambition as topics for discussion. The line manager acts as a trusted person and informal coach of the employee, while the human resources officer acts as the facilitator.

Managers and employees need to be encouraged to share their PBSC, to enable them to create an atmosphere of trust. Employees are responsible for their own development on the basis of their PBSC and the PDAC cycle and need to take the initiative themselves. This must focus on work as well as on spare time. A healthy home environment and a proper balance between work and private life is indispensable for better achievement at work. A way of life aligned with the PBSC and the PDAC cycle results in new challenges and the continuous development of related skills, whereby you will enjoy your work more and use your free time much better. The new task of managers and human resources officers is to improve the quality of life of employees on the basis of the PBSC method and the PDAC cycle, to have them take on greater challenges and through this increase work satisfaction and happiness. The quality of life of customers improves because of this, and they too will be happy and more satisfied. Managers and human resources officers should now understand that the influence of the home environment on work can no longer be ignored. Their new task is to stimulate the employees to start applying their PBSC systematically within their families as well, and improve the employees' family life on the basis of the PDAC cycle. After all, those who cannot function well in their own families cannot function well at work, either.

Business ethics is an essential part of the Personal Balanced Scorecard concept. This means that organizations must care about ethics and corporate social responsibility to ensure that their actions have integrity and reflect high ethical standards. The personal and shared ambitions should, therefore, be inspired by ethics. This will be discussed in Chapter 6.

To be able to move from strategy to action, it is necessary to link and communicate the OBSC to the BSC of departments and teams, as well as to individual performance plans of employees and managers on lower levels in the organization. Every participant in this process formulates his/her own PBSC. The ambition meeting between manager and employee, therefore, takes place on every level. On each organizational level, one needs to reflect on the balance between the personal ambition and the shared ambition of organization, department or team. It is therefore important to know at all levels which specific inner need hides behind the behavior of the people, and what motivates them to stay with the organization. The rolling out of the balanced scorecards gets special attention in Chapter 7.

To be able to manage and use the talents within the organization effectively, it is necessary to embed the personal and organizational balanced scorecards together in the talent management process. This is done on the basis of a new talent management model and a unique talent management cycle that consists of the following phases: Result Planning, Coaching, Appraisal and Talent Development. From an organizational perspective, this talent management cycle and individual capabilities is meshed with an organizational view of job capability requirements with the opportunity for talent development through assuming new responsibilities anywhere in the organization. This learning aspect is discussed in Chapter 8. In the final chapter, Chapter 9, I introduce the organic PBSC cycle, which is meant to be helpful for the successful implementation of the whole PBSC system. Figure 1.2 shows the correlation between Chapters 2 to 9.

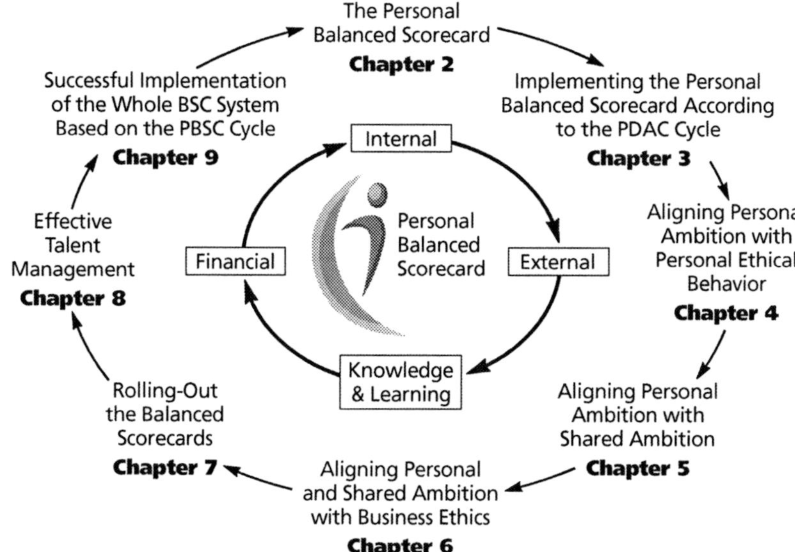

Figure 1.2. Correlations between Chapters 2 to 9

Appendix I describes the TPS Soft. This is a knowledge based and interactive heuristic software system that will assist you with the implementation of PBSC and Total Performance Scorecard. It offers management and HR the possibility to effectively steer their organization to greater performance, well-being, joy and motivation. Appendix II describes the TPS Life Cycle Scan which can be used to control the implementation of PBSC and Total Performance Scorecard. Based on the results of this self-assessment tool, companies can be TPS awarded and certified.

PART I

PBSC AS AN INSTRUMENT FOR INDIVIDUAL DEVELOPMENT, PERSONAL EFFECTIVENESS AND GROWTH IN LIFE

As long as we can put some idealism and reverence back on the global agenda, understanding that corporations and institutions have to be a force for positive change, then there is a light at the end of the tunnel. Over the past decade, while many businesses have pursued what I call "business as usual", I have been part of a different, smaller business movement ... We want a new paradigm, a whole new framework for making business a force for positive social change. It must not only avoid hideous evil—it must actively do good. I am not interested in business as usual. It is business as unusual that excites me.

—Anita Roddick, Founder of The Body Shop

CHAPTER 2

THE PERSONAL BALANCED SCORECARD

To live is to choose. But to choose well, you must know who you are and what you stand for, where you want to go and why you want to get there.

—Kofi Annan,
Secretary General, United Nations

The Personal Balanced Scorecard (PBSC) strikes a personal note in terms of self-examination. The changes in the thinking process and mindset which form its foundation are meant to prepare you for action and to stimulate your resolution, passion and energy so as to create inner involvement for work. By writing down your PBSC, you raise a mirror to yourself. On the basis of insights acquired through PBSC, you become more proactive, self-assured, smarter and faster learner. The PBSC encompasses personal mission, vision, key roles, critical success factors, objectives, performance measures, targets and improvement actions. These are divided into four perspectives: the internal, the external, the knowledge and learning, and the financial perspectives. It impacts your personal well being, and success at work and in the rest of life. The personal ambition (comprised of personal mission, vision and key roles) component allows you to express your

Personal Balanced Scorecard, pages 21–72

intentions, identity, ideals, values, and driving force, as well as to gain more insight about yourself. Ralph Waldo Emerson believed that—*"Personal ambition is the germ from which all growth of nobleness proceeds."*

Self-knowledge influences your attitude towards others as well as your emotional intelligence. After all, we do not know what it is that we don't know. Even worse, we do not even know that we don't know this. In the words of Socrates, *"The only true wisdom is in knowing you know nothing."* Similarly, Confucius has said—*"To know, is to know that you know nothing. That is the meaning of true knowledge."* When Jesus Christ was nailed to the cross, he said: *"Forgive them, as they know not what they do."* The people were ignorant. They lacked self-knowledge. By focusing inward and thinking about our actions—as undertaken through self-examination, we learn more and more about ourselves and therefore are able to function better. We learn not only more, but the truth about ourselves. As Thomas Huxley has said, *"Learn what is true in order to do what is right."* The words of Galileo Galilei may also be recalled here—*"You cannot teach a man anything; you can only help him discover it in himself."*

The theme of this chapter is to know and help yourself and others. I would like to point out ten reasons that form the basis for the PBSC.

First of all, it enables you to distance yourself from your mindset—the mental framework of assumptions and beliefs that colour your experience of the world—and to listen attentively to your inner voice. It also allows you to improve your behaviour and change your future course. This can be done in two ways; (1) by harmonizing external circumstances with your personal ambition and/or (2) to make changes in the way in which you experience external circumstances, so that they fit better within your personal ambition. Both strategies are part of the PBSC method. It has been proven in practice that if someone has a clear personal ambition, it will guide that person's life and will result in purposeful and resolute actions. Personal ambition includes a collection of challenges, targets and ethical starting points that form the context for your actions. By formulating your PBSC and through reflection on it through the breathing and silence exercises, you will get a better hold on your life as your self-awareness increases. Awareness is your inner voice that selectively chooses internal and external events for processing. Awareness consists of energy and information in the form of thoughts. As Abraham Maslow once said—*"What is necessary to change a person is to change his awareness of himself."*

Experience has shown that personal coaching in conformity with the PBSC allows people to discover themselves. In doing so, people are more willing to expand individual limits, and improve their attitudes by setting them in motion. Sir Winston Churchill has aptly said—*"Attitude is a little thing that makes a big difference."*

Formulating your personal ambition entails a search for your identity. And the key to action is understanding yourself. Through PBSC, you can master yourself and become more proactive, more disciplined, more effective and more responsible for yourself. It is your ethical duty and moral responsibility to develop yourself and become more proactive—not only for your own good, but also for your loved ones, your work, your organization, your country, and for the world that you are part of. Take the initiative. Do not blame others for your failures. Use the PBSC to coach and master yourself. For this, you only need yourself and someone close to you, whom you can trust, who listens effectively and gives you honest feedback; this person could be, for example, your spouse, manager, colleague or friend.

The second reason to apply the PBSC method involves working smarter instead of harder through learning and knowledge of the self. We become more creative as we grow more conscious of ourselves—our real character, inner processes and driving forces. To fathom your life, or to get a better self-image and greater self-knowledge, together with challenges, your learning ability gets greater. This leads to inner harmony. Through PBSC, you will be able to change your behavior, to unlearn bad habits and to let go of things. Change in behavior at the individual level results in collective behavioral change, which we call organizational change. The more innovative that an organization wants to be, the more its employees and managers should develop self-knowledge. A recent survey shows that many European managers have a skewed self-image (see the boxed text below). This has an enormously destructive impact on the health of their people and the organization. Without being aware of its effects, managers can cause disruptions in organizational functioning. Research in Europe shows that more than half of all employees have changed jobs or shifted organizations at least once because of their manager's behavior, and that mismanagement is the reason for their poor work performance (Bureau Interview NSS, 2004).

Applying the PBSC results in real learning. According to Peter Senge—

> Real learning gets to the heart of what it means to be human. Through learning we re-create ourselves. Through learning we become able to do something we never were able to do. Through learning we re-perceive the world and our relationship to it. Through learning we extend our capacity to create, to be part of the generative process of life. There is within each of us a deep hunger for this type of learning.

Self-knowledge or self-image includes self-awareness and *self-regulation.* Self-awareness is the ability to recognize and understand your strengths, weaknesses, needs, values, ambition, moods, emotions, and drives, as well as their effect on others. Self-regulation is the ability to control or redirect disruptive impulses, feelings, and moods. Self- awareness and self-regulation have an impact on self-confidence, trustworthiness, integrity, and

Managers Have a Skewed Self-Image

European managers think that they motivate, stimulate, and are attentive to their employees. On the contrary, their employees report experiencing an enormous lack of interest and stimulation on the job. This was proved by a study conducted by the Bureau Interview NSS in 2004 among 250 managing directors. The study shows a large difference between how managers think they lead and how employees experience it.86% of the managers feel that they show sincere interest, but only 41% of the employees agree; 84% of the managers are satisfied by their management strategy, but a mere 42% of the employees are satisfied with the way they are being led. Besides, 64% of managers feel that they are able to motivate themselves, while only 31% of the employees feel that their manager is able to do so. 83% of the managers feel they are accessible to their employees, but just 34% of the employees feel that their manager is ready to oblige them. Finally, 66% of managers feel that they know exactly what happens in their department, but only 32% of the employees agree.

openness to learn. It is an inner, spiritual learning process, which is related to both emotional and spiritual intelligence. This inner process starts with self-knowledge, or *knowing*. By *doing* or by routine application of the complete PBSC method, self-knowledge will lead to *wisdom*. Between knowing and wisdom lies an enormous distance which can be reduced by the complete PBSC system. We admire people who deliver top performances and find it exceptional. Anyone can increase their ability and deliver peak performances, because all of us have it within us to do so. Buddha has said that we should conquer ourselves. He said—*"Whoever won a thousand times from thousand armies, is nothing compared to someone who conquers himself."*

According to Lao-tzu, effective leadership comes from self-awareness and self-conquest. He said—*"He who knows other men is discerning; he who knows himself is intelligent. He who overcomes others is strong; he who overcomes himself is mighty ."* *Working smarter* is also related to the effective use of and the balance between the left and right side of your brain. This is one of the results of applying the PBSC method along with the breathing and silence exercise and the Plan–Do–Act–Challenge cycle. With the left half of your brain having mainly an analytical, logical and quantitative function, the right half of your brain has an intuitive and holistic function. Many people do not have a proper balance between the left and right sides of their brain. Most people only use the left side of their brain; because of this, they miss opportunities that allow them to become more adept at using the right hemisphere of the brain and to deal with complex problems in an integrated way. The personal mission, vision and key roles relate specifically to the right side of the brain, while the personal objectives, performance measures, targets and improvement actions within the PBSC have to do with the left side of the brain. The balance between these (i.e. between personal ambition and action) will be discussed later. Based on your PBSC, you will start acting intuitively thus making more effective use of the right side of your brain. Research has shown that top managers who believe in their intuition and make decisions intuitively are usually the most successful. (Agor, W., *Management by Consciousness*, Ed. G.P. Gupta, Sri Aurobindo Institute of Research in Social Sciences, Pondicherry, India, 1998.) In recent years I have applied the PBSC system in large companies in many countries, and have observed that this system has also a very positive affect on the self-awareness and self-regulation of people. People who have a high degree of self-awareness recognize how their feelings affect them, others, and their performance, they understand their clients, are honest, proactive, innovative, and goal oriented, speak openly, have self-confidence, and take calculated risks. People who have a high degree of self-regulation are able to create an environment of trust and fairness, can master their emotions, and are action oriented, trustworthy, and very effective in leading change.

The third reason is that finding the proper alignment between your personal ambition and your behavior results in personal integrity, inner peace, the expenditure of less energy, and the ability to be guided by your inner voice—all of which can lead to increased personal charisma. People with this perspective on life value others' lives and create a stable basis for others to feel they are credible. When you achieve this inner authority, you also have a positive effect on the loyalty, motivation, and dedication of those around you. In this book, I introduce an integral breathing and silence exercise, which will assist you in turning your attention inward, to give you control over your awareness and to let you think deeply. It actually actively trains the right half of your brain, thereby increasing your effectiveness. Henry Ford said, *"Thinking is the hardest work there is, which is probably the reason why so few engage in it."*

The fourth reason to apply the PBSC method is that if there is an effective balance between the interests of individual employees (personal ambition) and those of the organization (shared ambition), employees will work with greater commitment toward the development of their organization. The emphasis here lies on intrinsic motivation. *Intrinsic motivation is inherently pleasurable and it arises from within. People do something because they enjoy doing it* (Eleanor Lester, 2006). Development of the personal and organizational ambitions takes place simultaneously. When we answer the question of what we want for the organization and where we want to go together, we also ask what we want for ourselves and which situation accommodates both sets of interests best, so that it is win–win. Our behavior is driven by inner needs that arise from our experiences and mindsets. These needs and those of the organization must be aligned for the sake of higher productivity. Therefore, the work/life balance and a healthy home environment are indispensable for this. That is why this aspect is explicitly included in the PBSC method. A foundation is hereby created for a truly learning organization. In such a place, enjoyment will be stimulated by reducing the gap between company life and private life. Employees are increasingly looking to their workplaces to meet their social needs for recreation, fun, and friendship, and wish for it to be an extension of their family. They will work with dedication for something they believe in, which is interesting, exciting and ultimately a learning experience.

As Mihaly Csikszentmihalyi said,

> People, who learn to enjoy their work, and use their spare time the right way, often have the idea that their lives have become more valuable. The future is not only for the learned person, but also for the person who has learned to use his spare time effectively.

According to Roger Evans and Peter Russell—

> There is a kind of re-education needed to connect business management with normal life. There has always been an enormous gap between the way people treat colleagues at work and the way they treat friends and family. With regard to the latter, we do not see friendship, tolerance, etc. as sentimental and 'soft' when we deal with friends and family, but rather as a lubricant for the relationship. Could we not extend this to the business community as well? The gap between these two views is currently decreasing; perhaps here rests the solution for tomorrow's problems.

The fifth reason is that integration of the PBSC in the competence development process and establishing a connection with the Organizational Balance Scorecard (OBSC) results in effective talent management. This is related to continuously entering into challenging situations and developing related skills. Because of this, competence management in your organization does not turn into a cosmetic or a vague process, as is the case in many companies at the present time. On the basis of the integration of PBSC in this process, you will be able to effectively manage talents within your organization, and to put employees in a central position within the organization. Akito Morita, the creator of Sony, who treats his employees as member of his family declares—*"Machines and computers do not make business a success; it is the people. Similarly, no theory or plan will make business a success that can only be done with people."* Application of the PBSC system has also a positive affect on empathy, which is important for building and retaining talents, coaching and mentoring people, and leading teams. Empathy is the ability to understand the emotional makeup of other people. People who have a high degree of empathy can give effective feedback, are good coaches and mentors, and know how to reach top-performance.

The sixth reason to apply the PBSC method is to develop team learning. By stimulating individuals to share their personal ambitions with each other, they have a means to know, understand and appreciate each other better. Experience shows that because of this mutual trust and respect will grow. Routine implementation of the PBSC results in the adoption of a way of life characteristic of freedom.

According to Gary Jacobs—

> It is only under conditions of freedom that man will impose discipline upon himself and only self-discipline can create true personality growth.... The very act of giving freedom to a man in a new area serves as an incentive for him to extend his trust-worthiness to other areas. Freedom implies and compliments responsibility. If freedom is given it results in evolving a greater sense of and capacity for accepting responsibility.

The seventh reason to apply the PBSC is in order to use your time effectively. The aim is to become a highly disciplined time manager, by doing what you planned to do when you planned to do it. The PBSC is a plan for achieving your personal goals, actions, and priorities. It will help you to be ruthless with wasting time, and organize it more effectively. When something adverse happens or someone tries to pull you off course, you quickly return to your chosen path with the full knowledge that you are moving in the direction that you have stated in your PBSC.

The eighth reason is to drive out fear from the organization, by introducing an ambition meeting between line manager and employee. This meeting is periodic, informal, voluntary and confidential, with the employee's PBSC and the shared ambition as topic. The line manager functions here as a trusted person. This gives employees the feeling that they count for something. And that they are appreciated as human beings. This will create a firm foundation of peace and trust upon which creativity and growth can flourish.

The ninth reason is to reduce organizational stress and burnout. This happens through aligning the personal ambition with the shared ambition in concordance with the breathing and silence exercise introduced later. This exercise will give you energy and have a restful effect on you to produce a calm state of mind free from stress. Experience has shown that deeper involvement and harmonious working relationships created among employees through the PBSC method also reduces organizational stress and burnout. Public health scientists at UCL (England) have found that a happy state of mind can lead to a healthier heart and lower levels of stress-inducing chemicals.

The tenth reason to apply the PBSC method is to select the right candidate for the right job. The PBSC method can ensure the necessary job fit by matching the abilities, aptitude and motivation of the candidates with not just the job requirements but also with the shared ambition of the organization. The personal ambition of a candidate tells a better story than a resume. It is possible that a candidate seems suitable for a specific function on the basis of his/her CV, but if there is no match between his/her personal ambition and the ambition of the organization, this would not aid his/her performance. A good match between the job description and the personal ambition of the candidate therefore results in higher customer satisfaction. TPS Soft can guide you in this process (see Appendix I). The importance of recruitment in the areas of employee development and organizational success can be appreciated from the following observation of Akio Morita in his book entitled *Made in Japan*,

> In the long run, your business and its future are in the hands of the people you hire. To put it a bit more dramatically, the fate of your business is actually in the hands of the youngest recruit on the staff.

So don't waste any more time with personal and organizational development according to the traditional, more cosmetic approaches. Stop complaining and take the responsibility to develop a cheerful, vital and strong personality based on the PBSC.

Ten Ways in Which the Personal Balanced Scorecard Helps You Know and Help Yourself and Others:

1. By distancing yourself from your mindset and listening effectively to your inner voice, you are able to identify your inner strengths, gifts and personal goals and therefore create your future and discover your destiny.
2. Self-learning and working smarter instead of harder through learning and knowledge of the self. We become more creative as we grow more conscious of ourselves—our real character, inner processes and driving forces. This leads to inner harmony
3. Personal integrity; aligning and balancing your personal ambition with your personal behavior, you will create inner peace and improve your own credibility, as well as acting according to your conscience. The breathing and silence exercises will help turn your attention inward and to give you control over your self-awareness, self-regulation and empathy. When adopted as a habit, the breathing and silence exercises will develop a deep awareness of self at all times.

4. Enjoyment at work; as a result of the balance between your personal ambition and the shared ambition, your inner involvement is increased and more warmth within the organization is created. Happiness is enhanced at work by reducing the gap between company life and normal life, and between the way people deal with their colleagues at work and the way they act with their friends and family in their spare time.
5. Effective talent management; integration of the PBSC in the appraisal system results in a sustainable talent management process, which is related to a continued taking up of challenges and development of related skills.
6. Team learning and trust; to stimulate individuals to share their personal ambition with each other so that they get to know, understand and appreciate each other better, which forms a stable basis for greater mutual respect and trust.
7. Becoming a highly disciplined time manager by using your time effectively.
8. Driving out fear; the PBSC is a philosophy, which creates conditions to eliminate all fears of employees and enable them to realize their full potential and contribute creatively.
9. Reducing stress and burnout.
10. Recruiting employees effectively. To ensure the necessary job fit by matching the personal ambition with the job requirements and with the shared organizational ambition.

The PBSC allows you to reformulate your own ambition, objectives, principles, standards, and values and makes these available to you and to those you care for, to the benefit of the ideas you hold. Peter Senge has said that when an organization uses the personal ambition of its employees as a starting point, it becomes an instrument of self-realization, rather than a machine, which enslaves them. He points out that managers usually assume that encouraging employees to develop and express their personal ambition will only lead to organizational anarchy and confusion. However, it has been seen that these assumptions are unfounded, and that most employees are more than willing to align their personal ambition with their organization's ambition. Stephen Covey argues for an "inside out" approach. He explains that your starting point must be the core of your identity. In order to improve your relations with others, you must begin with having a better relationship with yourself. In other words, you must succeed in your personal life before you can achieve something in the world, and that you must be loyal to your self before you make promises to others. He has described it as a natural learning process, which through awareness of independence will lead to awareness of reciprocal dependence.

The elements of the PBSC are divided among various perspectives. These perspectives are of essential importance to your self-development, personal well-being, and success in society. They are, namely—

1. *Internal*—your physical health and mental state. How can you control these in order to create value for yourself and others? How can you feel good in your skin at work as well as in your spare time?
2. *External*—relations with your spouse, children, friends, employer, colleagues, and others. How do they see you?
3. *Knowledge and learning*—your skills and learning ability. How do you learn, and how can you remain successful in the future?
4. *Financial*—financial stability. To what degree are you able to fulfil your financial needs?

These four basic perspectives form an integral part of your personal mission, vision, key roles (which together form your personal ambition). The

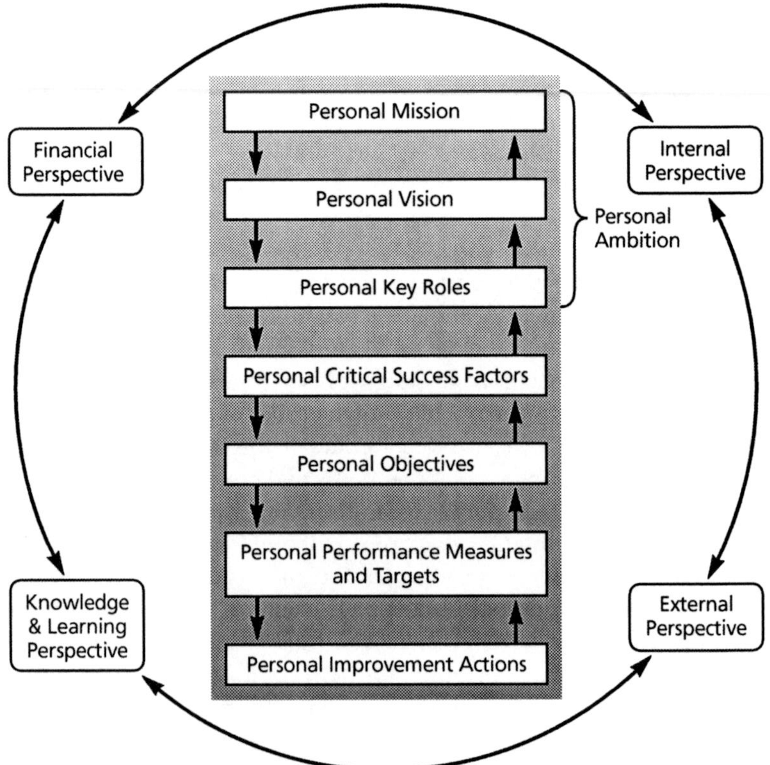

Figure 2.1. The Personal Balanced Scorecard Model (Rampersad, 2003)

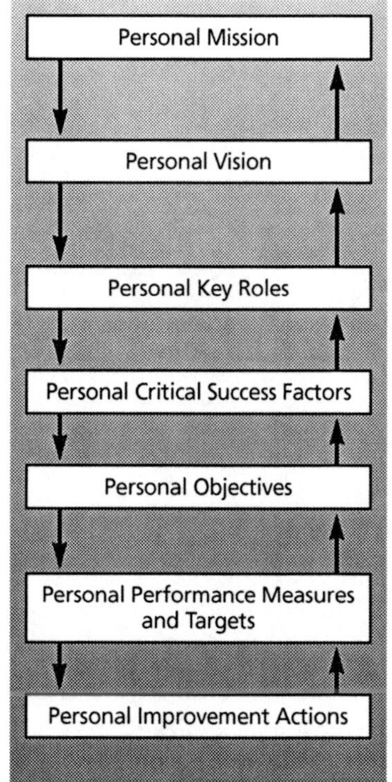

WHO AM I?
What is my philosophy of life? Why am I on this Earth? What are my overall life objectives? What do I live for? What are my deepest aspirations? Why do I do what I do? What are my unique talents? What are my core beliefs?

WHERE AM I GOING?
Which values and principles guide my way? What do I want to achieve? What are my long-term intentions? What is my ideal? What do I stand for? What do I believe in? How do I want to distinguish myself in society? How do I see myself?

WHAT TYPE OF RELATIONSHIP WOULD I LIKE TO HAVE WITH OTHERS?
How would I like to fulfill different roles in my life, in order to realize my personal mission and vision?

WHICH FACTORS MAKE ME UNIQUE?
Which factors in my personal ambition are decisive for my personal well-being and success? What are my most important competences?

WHICH RESULTS DO I WANT TO ACHIEVE?
Which measurable short-term personal results do I want to achieve? What are my most important shortcomings? What is the most important change I face regarding my work and career?

HOW CAN I MEASURE MY PERSONAL RESULTS?
What makes my personal objectives measurable? Which values do I have to obtain? What are my targets?

HOW DO I WANT TO ACHIEVE THE RESULTS?
How can I realize my personal objectives? Which improvement actions do I need to achieve this? How do I see to it that I learn continuously?

Figure 2.2. PBSC Framework (© Hubert Rampersad)

perspectives and the personal critical success factors together form the bridge between personal ambition and action. They link personal ambition (a long-term concern) and personal objectives, performance measures, targets and improvement actions (short-term factors). After all, ambition without action is hallucination. To turn ambition into action, you need energy. Energy is increased by habitually practicing the breathing and silence process. Figure 2.2 shows the questions, which form the basis of the PBSC.

The PBSC can be defined as the following formula:

PBSC = personal mission + vision + key roles + critical success factors + objectives + performance measures + targets + improvement actions (divided along the four perspectives: internal, external, knowledge & learning, and financial).

Figure 2.3 shows how these PBSC elements are related to each other. Every element in this formula will be explained later.

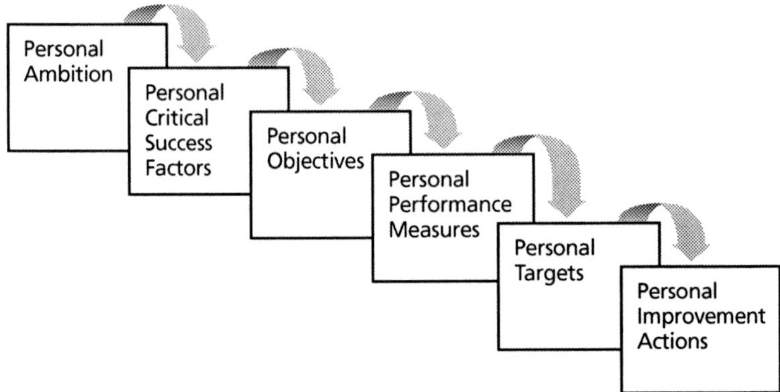

Figure 2.3. Relationship between PBSC Elements

PERSONAL AMBITION

> **Intuition**
>
> "Fully developed intuition is highly efficient—a way of knowing immediately. It is fast and accurate. Intuitive abilities will become more and more valuable during the coming period of surprises, complexities, and rapid changes. The organizations of tomorrow will require a breed of executives trained in these decision-making techniques. Successful executives tend to rely less on the fact-gathering and more on their instincts. Any time decisions must be made quickly or an issue is so complex that complete information is not available, the manager who have developed their intuition will have an advantage over those who have not. And in the rapidly changing, complex world of the future, these situations will be more and more common."
>
> —Weston Agor

You must have a personal ambition statement in life if you expect exceptional success. You will surely have it, since people who give their peak performance attract success. Keep the personal ambition you desire to achieve at the forefront of your mind each day. Personal ambition is simply a set of guiding principles which clearly state who you are, where you are going, where you want to be, etc. and which embodies your values. It is your personal lighthouse keeping you steadily on the course of your dreams. I have defined personal ambition as comprising of personal mission, vision, and key roles.

PERSONAL MISSION

Your personal mission statement encompasses your philosophy of life and your overall objectives, indicating who you are (the true you), why you are on this earth, your purpose in living, and your deepest aspirations. "Who am I?" is an identity question. It initiates a self-examination of your *personal identity* (the unique position you find yourself in) and a voyage of discovery. As Socrates, said—*"The unstudied life is not worth to be lived,"*

or,

"If you live without studying life, it is not worth calling it life."

Abraham Maslow expressed himself in this manner:

> There exists a personal "I" that which I sometimes call "listening to your intuitions." This means: letting your own I emerge. Most of us do not listen to ourselves but to the interrupting voice of others. You will discover that all knowledge is contained in life itself.

I also refer to Jesus Christ, who said—*"The Kingdom of God is within you."*

Swami Vivekananda reiterates this—*"The Kingdom of God is within us. He is there. Realize yourself. That is freedom. That is real worship."*

Inspired by them, Mahatma Gandhi said—*"Every person should listen to the voice of his conscience, be his own teacher and search inside himself the Kingdom of God. Who adheres to this, will not be kept down by any authority."*

Buddha's mission was to end human suffering. He found that the roots of suffering were in the human mind itself and not in the world. Bear in mind what he said—*"Your work is to discover your world and then with all your heart give yourself to it."*

Once you discover the core of your nature, your higher self, and know who you really are (your personal mission), you will find that it is possible to make every dream come true (your personal vision). Once you better understand who you are, it will be easier to channel your energy in the right direction, to achieve a dream which is worthy of your effort. By discovering and formulating your higher self, you will become visionary and will find out that you have something unique to offer. Your work is to find out what that is, and to work at it with passion. This process is closely related to *spirituality*. Spirituality is the manifestation of the perfection that is already present in you. It means realizing your inner essence. Religion is something external to you, whereas spirituality is something that is within you. Spirituality is needed in the modern world of business because it provides greater intuition to help in making tough decisions.

One of Deepak Chopra's spiritual laws of success is the law of the Dharma. Dharma is a Sanskrit word, which can be translated as "goal in life." This law has the following three components:

1. You are on this earth to discover your real "me," to find out that your real "me" is spiritual. This lies beyond your ego. Go look for it.
2. You possess unique talents, which no one else has. Discover them.
3. Use these talents to serve mankind.

Bill George (Medtronic Inc.) has this to say about ego:

> One of the things you have to do is to find a way to get egos out of the way, and it has to start with the CEO. People at the top of every large organization have strong egos. That's not just true of business. It exists in Congress, medicine, law.

Examples of Personal Mission Statements

- To create a world of love and empowerment, by loving and empowering others and myself.
- To be authentic and gracious, creating joy and deeper meaning in others' lives based on my uniqueness.
- To serve mankind as an ambassador of God by demonstrating how to perpetuate goodness and elevate the souls of all with whom I might interact.
- To serve the needs of mankind to the best of my ability by helping to build strong, viable organizations and guiding people to healthful and joyful living.

PERSONAL VISION

Your personal vision statement is a description of the way in which you want to realize your mission; your long-term dream. In Walt Disney's words, *"All our dreams can come true, if we have the courage to pursue them."*

Henry David Thoreau said—*"If a man advances confidently in the direction of his dreams to live the life he has imagined, he will meet with a success unexpected in common hours."*

Your personal vision describes where you want to go, the values and principles that guide you, what you stand for, what you want to achieve, the ideal characteristics you want to possess, your ideal job situation, and what you want to be. As William Shakespeare wrote—*"We know what we are, but know not what we may be."*

Your vision functions as an ethical compass, which gives meaning to your life. It is a concrete translation of your inner longings, and keeps in mind the four aforementioned perspectives. Your inner voice and convictions as to how life should play an important role in this. Your personal vision must result in purposeful actions and efforts to realize your dreams. It gives direction to your efforts. According to the Hindu scriptures known as the Vedas, personal vision is related to self-knowledge. The Buddhist concept of vision defines wisdom. Wisdom signifies that one clearly sees the nature of existence and the human situation in that context. The opposite of wisdom is ignorance. The Sanskrit word for ignorance is *avidya,* which means blindness. The Tibetan word for ignorance is *marigpa*, meaning unintelligence. According to Eastern philosophy visionary people are wise (knowledgeable) and people without a personal vision are blind and ignorant (unintelligent). Such ignorance may also be seen in people with wrong personal visions that result in useless deeds that create misery for themselves and others.

Your mission and vision have to do with your inner need and motives, as well as your self-awareness, imagination, and conscience. Through your conscience you realize what your principles are, which can be effectively rendered through your talents. Thus, you will be able to give direction to your life through your vision. It needs to be formulated in such a way that you will be stimulated to reflect on your life and on everything you undertake. Stephen Covey says that you can gain insight about your personal ambition if you can answer two questions: 'What would you like to have engraved on your tombstone?; and 'Which memories would you like to leave behind after your death?' In other words, what would you like people to say about you after your death and what difference would it have made if you had lived. In Table 2.1 you will find seemingly easy questions, which are nevertheless central to your sense of self. These questions relate to *being* and *becoming*. Imagine stepping outside of your physical body, taking a look at the real you, and asks yourself some of these ambition questions. Listen carefully to the answers of your inner voice.

Table 2.1. Primary Questions That Are Central to Your Personal Mission and Vision (Rampersad, 2003)

Personal Mission *(BEING)*	***Personal Vision*** *(BECOMING)*
Who am I?	Where am I going?
What is my philosophy of life?	Which values and principles guide my way?
Why am I on this earth?	What do I want to help realize?
What are my overall life objectives?	What do I want to achieve?
What do I live for?	What are my long-term intentions?
What are my deepest aspirations?	What is my ideal?
Why do I do, what I do?	What do I stand for?
What are my unique talents?	What do I believe in?
Where do I stand now?	Which contribution to society do I strive to make?
What are my core beliefs?	How do I want to distinguish myself in society?
What do I think about myself?	How do I see myself (self-image and self-valuation)?
What do I enjoy most?	How do I treat others?
What makes me happy?	

Examples of Personal Vision Statements

Example 1

I want to realize my mission in the following manner:

1. Function as partner to my internal and external customers and to add value for them
2. Always keep my physical and mental condition in good shape
3. Continuously develop my professional abilities
4. Experience enjoyment in my work by being full of initiative and to keep on learning
5. Create a work-life balance
6. Retain financial stability

Example 2

I want to realize my mission in the following manner.

1. Always act and serve out of love
2. Continuously pay attention to optimize my spiritual development, my emotional balance and physical health
3. Control my learning process purposefully, and, on this basis, be intuitive and creative
4. Develop my moral character and personal integrity
5. Keep my financial independence

Example 3

I want to realize my mission like this.

1. Keep developing my knowledge and strive for perfection
2. Continuously go into what fascinates my fellow men
3. Be honest to others and myself
4. Enjoy physical, emotional and mental health
5. Have financial security in order to realize personal freedom

The four basic perspectives—*internal, external, knowledge & learning, and financial*—are clearly recognizable in these examples. These perspectives must be an integral part of personal ambition in order to be able to formulate the PBSC completely. They are identified as critical success factors in personal ambition and after that, translated in the PBSC into personal objectives, performance measures, targets and improvement actions.

The vision of Bill Gates 30 years ago was—a PC on each desk in each house. Recently he said, *"When I was 19, I saw the future and based my career on what I saw. I have been right."*

Konosuke Matsushita, one of Japan's greatest entrepreneurs, admitted that his futuristic personal vision was responsible for his success—*"I have tried to envisage intuitively rather than analytically, the changes that will occur in our society and I have tried to create what life will be in the next century."*

His triumph was the balancing of Western rationalism with the spiritualism of the East. The personal vision of Joanne Kathleen Rowling was—I want to become a writer. She has become one of the most successful authors in history, thanks to the success of the Harry Potter books. The personal vision of Henry Ford was:

> I will build a motor car for the great multitude... constructed of the best materials, by the best men to be hired, after the simplest designs that modern engineering can devise... so low in price that no man making a good salary will be unable to own one—and enjoy with his family the blessing of hours of pleasure in God's great open spaces.

Henry Ford was the first to introduce the assembly line in 1914, and to mass produce cars. The price of cars then dropped, which made them affordable for the general public. Until 1920, Ford had the largest and fastest factory in the world.

PERSONAL KEY ROLES

Your key roles relate to the way you wish to fulfil the many essential roles in your life and thus realize your personal mission and vision. What type of relations would you like to have with your colleagues, friends, family, neighbours, and others? The formulation of your key roles will also result in greater self-knowledge and a better self-image, which in turn improves your learning ability. According to Stephen Covey, your personal ambition is an individualized constitution on which your life and behavior are based. This in turn forms the basis for determining your decisions about what you want to achieve. They involve your inner needs and motives as well as your self-consciousness, power of imagination, and conscience. On this basis, you will be able to give direction to your life. G.P. Gupta believed that

> Consciousness is the "inner aspect" of life. It's made up of two elements: (1) awareness of self and things, (2) forces and conscious power. Awareness is the first necessity; you have to be aware of things in the right consciousness, in the right way, seeing them in their truth. But awareness by itself is not enough. There must be a Will and Force that make the consciousness effective.... If one changes one's consciousness the whole world itself changes for you.... Based on consciousness, management has to be developed "Within-to-Without."

Examples of Personal Key Roles

- *Spouse:* To be happy together, to do fun things, to stimulate each other and enjoy it. To build a future together, in which I give and receive love, show respect and give trust.
- *Husband:* My wife is the most important person in my life.
- *Mother:* A support for my children on which they can fall back, and to be there while they strive towards a happy life.
- *Father:* To guide my children on the road to independence. To help them get the most out of the possibilities which their body and soul have to offer.
- *Daughter:* To give and receive love from my parents and to learn from their wisdom in life.
- *Sister:* To share and do things together.
- *Girlfriend:* To trust that which will never be damaged.
- *Friend:* My friends can always count on me, I will never disappoint them.
- *Colleague:* To work for successes with my colleagues, to share knowledge and to ensure that there is an open and harmonious working atmosphere. I will make sure that my colleagues see me as a trustworthy and knowledgeable person.
- *Student:* I learn something every day. I will always to some extent remain a student.
- *Manager:* To help make the organization for which I work successful and through this, serve the community.
- *Coach:* To bring others in contact with their spiritual truth and to assist them in their development.
- *Advisor:* To help my customers attain their goals.
- *Interim manager:* To assist organizations in achieving top performance.

Key roles have to do primarily with the external perspective in the PBSC. Elements from the key roles should also be identified as critical success factors and then be translated in the PBSC to personal objectives, performance measures, targets and improvement actions.

CRITERIA FOR PERSONAL AMBITION STATEMENTS

Personal ambition statements are most effective when they comply with the following criteria—

- Personal mission is aimed at the *being*, and personal vision at *becoming*.
- The four perspectives—financial, external, internal, and knowledge and learning—are a part of it.
- The emphasis is on selflessness; this brings the best results. Swami Vivekananda said—*"Unselfishness is more paying. Only people do not have*

the patience to practise it..., Unselfishness is more paying from the point of view of health also." Service brings with it the pure joy of self-giving: the highest level of motivation is providing service to another.

- Personal ambition is specific to each person and includes ethical starting points, with an emphasis on skills, principles, values, and standards (such as integrity, reliability, trust, helpfulness, credibility, frankness, teamwork). Integrity, which means the discipline to live according to your inner truth, is a concept that often appears in personal mission statements.
- Personal mission is short, clear, simple, and formulated in the present tense; it is concrete and may be used as a guideline.
- Personal mission and vision are unique for each person and are recognizable as such to others.
- Personal mission and vision are formulated positively, in an arresting manner, and are durable. The mission is not time-bound, while the vision is (approx. ten years).
- Personal mission and vision are both formulated in the present tense.
- Personal vision is ambitious and inspiring; it gives direction to personal initiative and creativity, and combines personal power and energy. It must result in purposeful effort and action to make the vision come true. Vision without the energy to act is meaningless. The breathing exercise below will assist you in developing energy.
- Personal vision is directive; it takes care of inner guidance and determines today's actions in order to reach the most desired future.
- Personal vision indicates how a person wants to distinguish himself or herself in society.
- Personal vision is based on self-image, self-knowledge, self-acceptance, and self-development; it requires a positive image of ourselves and of others. The biggest hindrance in creating our vision and mission is our own thinking. Ordinarily, we do not really think about ourselves, and we are blocked by our mindset. That is why I am introducing an integrated breathing and silence exercise, which will assist in removing these obstacles.
- Personal ambition can be made visual with a drawing or a metaphor, and is focused on work and life.

PRACTICAL CASE: THE PERSONAL AMBITION OF FRED ENGEL BASED ON A METAPHOR

Personal ambition can also be visualized as a metaphor. This is illustrated by Fred Engel's personal ambition, which is based on the logo of TPS International Inc. The logo of TPS International Inc., related to the Total Performance Scorecard (TPS) concept, is a stylized form of a surfer (see Figure 2.4).

Figure 2.4. Logo of TPS International Inc.

The sport of surfing is one with a lot of dynamism and perseverance, and also one that brings continuous challenges, a constant process aimed at working in tandem with nature—which requires being attuned to the form and the movement of the waves. TPS is also an ongoing and continuous process of aligning your personal ambitions with the direction of your 'surf board' and with the movements of your organization.

Surfers try to keep themselves upright as much as they can despite the movements of the water, looking for the right wave, and try to anticipate its height and speed. Although unexpected developments occasionally occur, in general they know how to foresee this, and plan for where the next wave develops and the power with which it will increase, as well as how to use it to bring them closer to shore—because getting safely to shore is their personal ambition. They need to use the (sometimes hostile) waves to achieve this, and therefore need to align their personal ambition with the sea's (the organization's) ambition. It is a form of staying in control within a

Exercise: Formulate Your Personal Ambition

Try to discover yourself, and then with all your heart give yourself up to that and do what is right. Sit down and:

1. Draft a statement (around 1.3 sentences) of your personal mission.
2. Draft a related statement of your personal vision.
3. Formulate your key roles; define the types of relationship you would like to have with your trusted friends, family, neighbours, and others.
4. Make sure that all four perspectives are included in your personal ambition.
5. If you use a trusted person as a personal coach, allow this person to help you with the breathing and silence exercise, to ask/discuss the ambition questions leading to your personal mission, vision and key roles and let him/her give you inspiration and motivation for the realization of your PBSC. Meet with him/her regularly, listen to him/her, and take his/her counsel.

larger system than you, by combining your skills with the momentum of the larger system's development—the surf, the organization, and society.

My personal ambition is to communicate and to share my faith and belief in God. For me, this surfing is a visualization of my personal ambition, where the surf stands for society—a society that has developments of varying predictability; a society that I need to fulfil my personal ambition, notwithstanding its sometimes "hostile waves"; a society in which many are experimenting with spiritual experiences (a sign that spirituality is becoming more and more important), through religion or otherwise, and I need to use this movement, this momentum, this wave. At the same time, I also need to stay in balance with society (the surf) to reach the beach.

AN INTEGRATED BREATHING AND SILENCE EXERCISE

The life of inner peace, being harmonious and without stress, is the easiest type of existence.

—Norman Vincent Peale

By paying attention to your own thoughts by way of a breathing and silence exercise, you can discover your identity and you will be able to distance yourself from your mindset. Through this exercise, you learn to look at life with new eyes, and can perceive what goes on within you. Because of this, you will know where you stand in life. Formulating your personal ambition can serve as a crowbar to pry off your rusty prejudices which block your creativity. You will be better equipped to create your future and discover a destination for yourself. After all, only if you know yourself will you be able to discover your talents and develop your personal goals. Then you can put them to the service of yourself and others. Vivekananda said—*"The greatest force is derived from the power of thought. Thought makes our body. Whatever we think we become. Pure and elevated thought makes us pure."*

In Buddha's words, *"We are what we think with our thoughts. We make the world."* It is therefore important to listen to your inner voice—it tells you what is best for you and how you can control your inner processes. An important rule here is: listen effectively to yourself, trust your inner voice, and obey it. You will then act with conviction. In this regard, Selvarajan Yesudian, the Indian yoga guru, says

> Let us make it our habit to constantly focus our attention inwardly and dwell within ourselves. Then we build our house on sturdy ground and not on quicksand. Looking from the safe height of our heart we can observe our own development, our growth, and the expansion of our awareness without losing our inner peace. This way, we'll be able to understand and accept every situation we experience and every phase of development we go through.

Breathing and silence exercises will assist you in turning your attention inward and in gaining control over your awareness. They help in bringing the left and the right side of your brain in balance. Breathing and thinking ability arise from the same center. Once breathing control is achieved, thought control follows and vice versa. The mind is intimately connected with breathing. When your mind is agitated, your breathing becomes quick and shallow. When you are relaxed and focused, your breathing is deep and calm. Breathing unites body and soul. According to Sri Sri Ravi Shankar, breathing is the link between body, thinking and emotions. Every emotion results in a certain breathing pattern. When you pay attention to your breathing, you will find that your thoughts and emotions relax. Breathing plays an important role also by removing anger from your thoughts and body. Because of the breathing exercise, your breathing becomes deeper, more regular and slower resulting in a restful effect on you.

Breathing and relaxation are inextricably connected. Proper breathing creates a good basis for physical and mental health. After all, when we breathe, we take in oxygen. Most people breathe quickly, superficially and uneasily, only using one-third of their lung capacity. A life energy deficiency results in a low energy level, coupled with stuffiness and listlessness. A surplus of life energy makes you cheerful and strong, lets you relax and results in a positive attitude, free from stress. You need life energy to set your personal ambition in action.

The silence exercise is a form of meditation. The Bible says, "*Be silent, and know I am God.*" This state can only be reached through meditation. Silence can be thought of as a synonym for meditation. It is the most effective way of communication. The Westerner often has a distorted view of meditation, arising out of ignorance and blindness. Meditation is a state that creates clarity and gives you a direct experience of your spirit. The spirit, according to Buddha, is a combination of feelings, observations, thoughts and sensory awareness. During meditation, your spirit has a chance to settle down and relax, to develop awareness and to aid in acting more effectively. Your spirit decides, for the most part, about how you act and in what state of mind you are. Meditation includes the re-discovery of a natural state of awareness and forms an effective basis for your self-knowledge. Meditation does not mean concentration, but a deep state of relaxation, letting go, calmness, a high state of awareness, mental strength, inner peace, enjoyment and satisfaction. Concentration is the result of meditation. This happens through your enhanced mental power and awareness and a calmer spirit. A calmer state of mind leads to clear thinking, which results in more creativity, less waste of energy and a holistic view of reality. This is really necessary in order to implement your PBSC effectively. There are other advantages of meditation—because of a calmer spirit, one has lower blood pressure and heart beat, the ability to better deal with stress, and controlling of pain, etc. All of us have human values; because of stress and tension they are not visible. Meditation makes them visible. There is evidence that people who meditate regularly live longer than those who do not. Recent experiments conducted at the Institute of HeartMath provide evidence that increasing physiological coherence also improves cognitive performance (Rollin McCraty, 2002). The more coherent or in sync we are, the better our cognitive performance.

Meditation makes it possible to look at the world through the glasses of our thoughts. It assists you in observing and accepting your thoughts and feelings. During meditation, let your thoughts come and go; this includes the thoughts in regard to your personal ambition, such as who you are, where are you going, etc. This silent process makes it easy to answer ambition questions, and because of it, your ambition statement becomes more effective. These questions are connected to your inner voice and enable you to discover the truth about yourself and your life. Formulating your personal ambition is primarily done by transcribing your inner voice after contemplating a couple of probing questions (which will be discussed later in this chapter). Although this voice is present in all of us, it cannot always be heard because: (1) most of us are not capable of hearing this voice because we are too focused on the outside world; and (2) the inner voice is drowned out by the noise around us. To hear your inner voice you must tune into the same wavelength in which your spirit communicates with yourself.

Brainwaves During Breathing and Silence Exercise

During the breathing and silence exercise, you produce brainwaves. These are like small electric currents in your head, which are of different measurable frequencies. The lower the frequency, the more inwardly directed your attention is. This is related to increased relaxation and inner peace. Anna Wise (1995) distinguishes the following four brainwave areas (see Figure 2.5):

- *Beta waves;* these waves have a frequency of 14–38 Hz (frequency in Hertz = number of vibrations per second). You are actively aware of the outside world. You are unable to concentrate during this stage of the exercise. Relaxation exercises calm the beta waves.
- *Alpha waves;* these waves have a frequency of 8–14 Hz. They are associated with relaxation and increase as you turn your attention more inward.
- *Theta waves;* these waves have a frequency of 4–8 Hz. These brainwaves are related to creativity, inspiration, dreams, and storage of memories in the long-term memory.

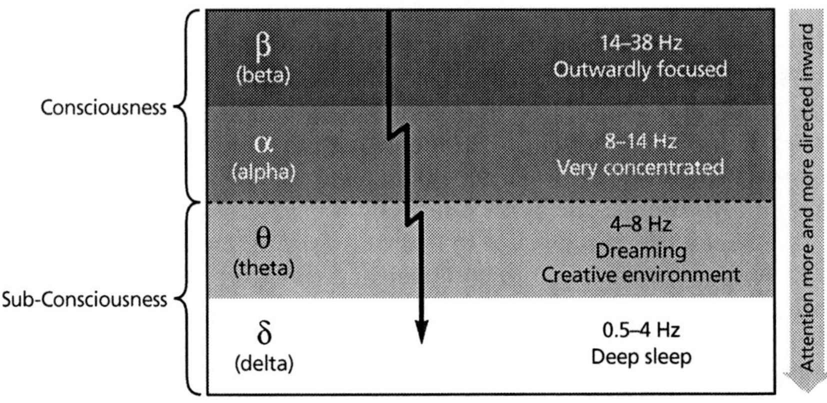

Figure 2.5. Brain Waves during Breathing and Silence Exercises

- *Delta waves;* these waves have a frequency of 0.5–4 Hz. These waves are produced primarily during deep sleep. These waves are related to empathy and intuition.

There are several forms of breathing and silence exercises. In the following boxed text, I introduce a simple integrated breathing and silence exercise, which has proven to be very effective. Performing this breathing and silence exercise for 20 minutes early in the morning and 20 minutes in the evening will give exceptional results if regularly practiced for six months.

An Integrated Breathing and Silence Exercise (© Hubert Rampersad)

Step 1: Breathing Exercise

1. Look for a quiet spot with fresh air and make sure that you will not be disturbed.
2. Sit in a comfortable chair with an upright back, and keep your back straight, and your shoulders and neck relaxed.
3. Gently rest your hands on your knees, with your palms upward and shut your eyes.
4. Breath deeply through your nose according to the following rhythm: inhale deeply during a count to four (your stomach fills like a balloon), hold your breath during four counts, and exhale fully during a count of six (your stomach flattens again) and stop for a count. Focus on the rhythm of breathing in and out.
5. Focus your attention entirely on your breathing during this process and observe how your life energy flows through your body. During the breathing you will become more relaxed. Concentrate on the feeling of relaxation in your whole body (face, shoulders, hands, feet, etc.).

6. Repeat this process during 10 minutes.

It is very important that you breathe through your nose. Because of this, your breath will be preheated and deeper.

Step 2: Silence Exercise

1. After finishing the breathing exercise, remain in your sitting position with your back straight, relax your arms, keep your eyes closed and breathe normally through your nose.
2. Focus entirely on your thoughts; do not concentrate on anything else. If thoughts do enter, do not force them out but simply let them pass like clouds making way for the beautiful blue sky.
3. Allow your thoughts to come and go, including the thoughts related to your personal ambition questions. Simply think about who you are, why you are on this earth, what is important to you in your life, etc.
4. Be open to all images that come up in your mind. Imagine that you are in a garden and that a wise man approaches you who, after introducing himself, asks you some of the ambition questions mentioned in the following page. Listen carefully to the answers of your inner voice.
5. Open your eyes after 10 minutes slowly and write the answers of your inner voice in a silence diary. The purpose of this diary is to be able to use this information to formulate or update your Personal Balanced Scorecard and keep record of your experiences and progress in each session.

Ambition Questions

- Who am I? What is my identity? Why am I on this earth? Why am I here?
- What is my self-image? How do I see myself?
- What kind of person am I? What do I stand for? What do I believe in?
- Which values and principles are closest to my heart, are sacred to me, and are rooted most deeply in my life? For example: honesty, helping others, self-development, expertise, money, enjoyment, affection, working together pleasantly, getting respect, status, etc.
- Which of these values clash with each other and with my strong sides?
- What is good and what is bad?
- What do I enjoy the most? Will I enjoy this in the future as well?
- How do I create meaning in my life and see to it that everything is not about earning money?
- To what extent is material wealth important to me?
- Where do I stand and where do I want to go? Where would I like my life to be headed?
- How and what do I want to be? What do I hope to become? In the broadest sense, what do I want to achieve with my life? What do I live for?

- What future would I like to have? What constraints stand in the way of realizing that future? What weaknesses do I have to deal with those constraints?
- What prevents me from being who I want to be and what I want to be?
- What is my purpose in life?
- How do I want to know myself and be known to others?
- If I die, what legacy would I like to leave behind, and what would I like to have meant to others?
- What difference will it have made that I existed?
- What do others say about me? What do I think about others?
- Where would you want to be at the end of your life?
- What are my ambitions and deepest aspirations about the community in which I want to live? What do I want to help realize?
- What do I most want to learn? Which habits would I like to unlearn? What do I very much like to do? What do I think is very important? What do I find nice and attractive? What am I willing to sacrifice to realize my objectives? What do I really want?
- What do I want to invest in life and what do I want to gain from it?
- How would I prefer my daily life to be?
- What gives me satisfaction?
- What makes me happy or sad?
- In which kind of environment do I prefer to be?
- How is my health?
- What are the five best qualities of individuals who I admire?
- To what extent are spiritual values important to me? What do I think of religion?
- Who are the most important persons in my life? What is my relationship to them?
- How do I connect with my life companion, friends, family, colleagues, and others?
- Why did I go to work for my present employer?
- How am I at work?
- Why do I do what I do? What is the importance of what I do?
- What am I good at and what not? In what did I fail? What are my biggest failures?
- What are my problems? What are the effects of my problems on my relationships with others? What effects have the problems on my physical health?
- When I was happy, what made me so happy?
- What have I done up till now, and what have I achieved?
- What is difficult for me to give up in my private, social, and business life?
- Which social questions intrigue me? Which social contributions would I like to make?

- What do I want to be in my organization? What am I trying to achieve? What is keeping me back?
- How can I serve mankind?
- Which contribution am I trying to make to the realization of my organizational ambition?
- What are the most important motivators in my job?
- To which job do I aspire? What are my wishes? What do I strive for? What are my concerns?
- What is happening to my profession, material possessions, family, life companion, friends, and others?
- Why am I active in a certain club?
- Will the things mentioned above still be important to me ten years from now?

If you use a trusted person as a personal coach, allow this person to help you with the breathing and silence exercise by:

1. Counting softly
2. Reminding you to allow your thoughts to come and go
3. Reminding you to think about a wise person who asks several of the ambition questions, and to pausing between the questions to allow time for thought.
4. Helping you with the selection of the ambition questions
5. Helping you to keep record of your experiences and progress during the exercise.
6. Helping you to finalize your PBSC.
7. Giving you feedback.

All these seemingly simple ambition questions are difficult to answer, when people are not open, who do not want to make an effort to find out what they want from their life and are blind to it. The breathing and silence exercise is meant to create an atmosphere of silence and inner peace, so that you will be able to answer these questions. By doing these exercises for 10–20 minutes (later to be expanded to 50–60 minutes), you will be able to achieve a lot of things on your own. This exercise allows you to think deeply about yourself and makes you aware of yourself and your core beliefs. By questioning yourself and listening intently to your inner voice, which systematically answers the above questions for you, you will be able to discover and change your obstructive beliefs. By doing this, you will gain more insight into the workings of your mind and the influence this has on your personal behavior, thought, and learning ability. Through this you can also accomplish the following—

- To enable you to come into contact with your self, and to clarify your personal ambition, and the human values within you.
- To reach a mental state wherein you can forget about yourself and feel happy.

- Increase your personal effectiveness and deliver mind-expanding performances.
- Discover your subconscious motives and through this get more out of yourself and coach yourself effectively.
- Understand your thoughts better and thus control your inner conflicts (between feelings and reason) better, and come in contact with your inner truth.
- Deal with your environment with greater inner peace, harmony, self-confidence, and involvement.
- Create positive energy and utilize this effectively for the sake of yourself and others.
- Make optimum use of your personal abilities and capabilities, and eliminate annoying behavior.
- Think and act more proactively, deal with your attitude in a more conscious way, and create a positive atmosphere.
- Deal better with emotions, stress, and burnout.
- Divide your attention more satisfactorily between work, hobbies, and family.
- To improve your personal learning style, as well as your self-awareness, self-discipline and consciousness and about self-responsibility.
- Formulate and implement your PBSC effectively.

PERSONAL CRITICAL SUCCESS FACTORS

The personal Critical Success Factors (CSFs) are derived from the personal ambition. They are related to the four perspectives, internal, external, knowledge and learning, and financial. A personal ambition without these four perspectives results in an incomplete PBSC. The personal CSFs form the bridge between the personal ambition (long term) and on the other side the personal objectives, performance measures, targets, and improvement actions (short term). This link is made by identifying your personal core competencies in your personal ambition related to the four perspectives. These personal CSFs will then be translated into concrete personal objectives. A personal ambition, therefore, has a minimum of four CSFs (at least one per perspective), and every CSF has one or more related personal objectives; each objective has a maximum of two related performance measures, while each performance measure has only one related target; each target is linked to one or more related improvement actions. The CSFs form milestones that can be realized. They are factors, which make you unique and in which you can further develop yourself and make a difference. Some examples of personal CSFs are—financial stability, good physical and mental health, and professional ability. The crucial questions here

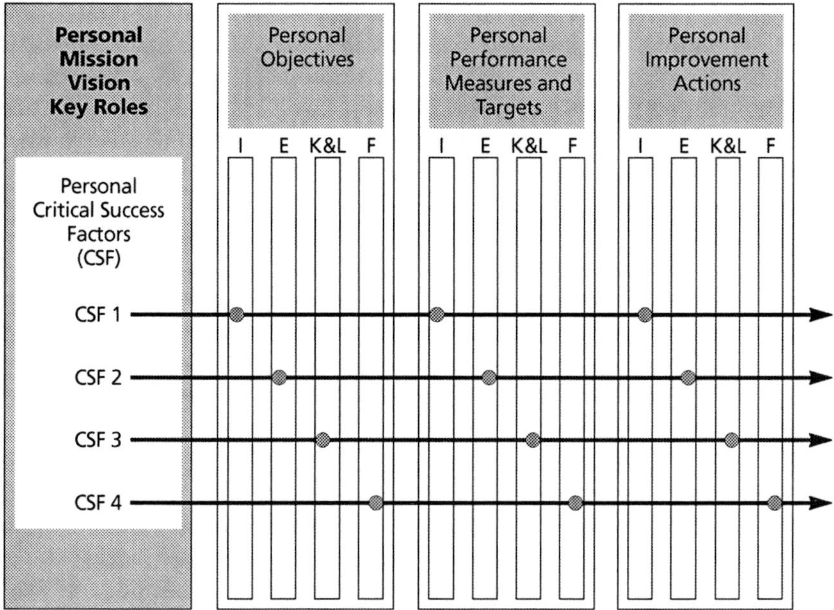

Figure 2.6. Each Personal CSF is Related to Personal Objectives, Performance Measures, Targets, and Improvement Actions

are—which factors make me unique? What determines my success? Which factors in my personal ambition are important for my wellbeing? Which factors in my personal ambition are essential for the realization of my objectives? What are my most important competencies? Figure 2.6 illustrates how the CSFs in the PBSC are linked according to each perspective, to the objectives, performance measures, targets, and improvement actions.

PERSONAL OBJECTIVES

The central question here is—"Which measurable short-term personal results do I want to achieve?" Personal objectives describe a result that you want to achieve in order to realize your personal ambition. Your personal ambition is aimed at the long-term future and your personal objectives at the short-term. The personal CSFs form the bridge between these. Your personal objectives are derived from your personal CSFs and from an analysis of your strengths and weaknesses. Each personal CSF has one or more personal objectives that are related to one of the four scorecard perspectives. The objectives can be quantified through personal performance measures and targets. Personal objectives provide you with the criteria needed to discuss, monitor, and evaluate your performance. It specifies short-range and long-range objectives of personal importance. Personal objectives are stated in clear, concise, specific, result-oriented, challenging but realistic, relevant, and cost effective terms. Performance measures and targets make this measurable and bound by deadlines.

A personal SWOT analysis forms the basis of your personal objectives. Make a list of all your strengths and weaknesses. You have to acknowledge things, which you are not good at. Weaknesses also include habits that restrict you, have an unfavorable influence on your life and deliver poor results. It is also important to focus on things in which you are accomplished, so as to make your performance even better. When analyzing your strengths, ask yourself the following questions—what are some of the strengths that have contributed to my success up to the present? How might these create problems for me in the future? Which problems would I like to solve first? While analyzing your shortcomings, you should think about the following questions—what do you think are your biggest shortcomings? Has anyone ever mentioned any of these shortcomings to you? Can you describe a situation where any of these shortcomings would be a serious handicap? You could also ask yourself this question—what is the most important challenge I face regarding my work and career? Factors that may be related to these questions are, for example, aptitude, talent, ability, intelligence, goal-orientation, perseverance, self-control, health, integrity, creativity, tolerance, enthusiasm, the home and work environments, responsibility, job prestige, status, power, freedom, having more free time, and so on. Some examples of personal objectives could be—appreciation from customers, improved leadership skills, inner peace, and greater knowledge. Your objectives could be to develop a dynamic, charismatic personality and to become a highly competent, strong, disciplined, calm and decent individual. Each month set a physical fitness objective for you. You cannot do good and be more productive, creative and dynamic unless you feel good and are relaxed and fit.

Personal Performance Measures

Personal performance measures are standards to measure the progress of your personal objectives. With it, you can assess your functioning in relation to your personal critical success factors and objectives. Without performance measures and targets, it is difficult to coach yourself with feedback. Performance measures urge you to action if they are related to your objectives, giving you a certain direction. They measure the changes, and compare this with the norm, and thus, in time, give you information about steering yourself. It is recommended that you define a maximum of two performance measures per objective. This section of the PBSC deals with the following questions—how can I measure my personal results? What makes my personal objectives measurable? Table 2.2 shows an overview of possible personal performance indicators according to each PBSC perspective.

Table 2.2. Examples of Personal Performance Measures per BSC Perspective (Rampersad, 2005)

Perspective	*Personal Performance Measures*
Internal	• level of being inspired
	• level of tension
	• level of stress
	• level of immunity to stress
	• level of enjoyment
	• level of laughing
	• level of trust from my manager
	• number of times I act with consideration versus acting without consideration
	• number of times that I feel good in my skin
	• number of times that I feel frustrated in my work
	• level when I am irritated at work
	• level of joy going to work
	• number of hours jogging
	• percent of mental absence
	• body weight
	• number of hours sleep
	• frequency of sporting
	• number of new challenges
	• number of uncontrolled emotions at work
	• number of times being mad
	• hours physical rest
	• percent of sick leave
	• number of times fitness
	• frequency breathing and silence exercise
	• number of cigars per day
	• fat contents
	• number of km per month on a bicycle
	• number of stomach muscle exercise
	• number of times per month playing golf
	• fitness score
	• cholesterol level
	• number of times feeling full of energy
	• percent of my life in positive shape

Table 2.2. Examples of Personal Performance Measures per BSC Perspective (Rampersad, 2005) (Cont.)

Perspective	*Personal Performance Measures*
	• number of times intuitive impulses • alcohol consumption • percent safety incidents • number of times at a psychologist • physical condition • my delivery speed • number of processing mistakes • throughput time of my work • response time to a service request • percent delayed orders
External	• degree of customer satisfaction • number of activities with the children • number of times doing something together • number of donations per year • reliability of my services • number of successful acquisition meetings • number of appreciating and loving remarks from spouse • level of satisfaction of others with regard to my actions • perception score from others with regard to my cooperation with them • level of satisfaction of my customers • number of warnings from my manager • number of productive hours at my work • number of positive changes initiated by me • number of times positive feedback received from my clients, manager and colleagues. • availability • accessibility • number of open and good conversations with loved ones • number of committee functions in social organizations • number of satisfied customers • level in which I feel that I have been of added value • number of complaints from internal and external customers • number of hours quality time with my family • number of family outings • number of arguments with my spouse • number of good conversations with my loved ones • percent of personnel who find they are working under effective leadership • percent of colleagues that consider me to be a good colleague • number of times given assistance to others • number of times positive feedback related to my ethical behavior

Table 2.2. Examples of Personal Performance Measures per BSC Perspective (Rampersad, 2005) (Cont.)

Perspective	*Personal Performance Measures*
	• customer valuation score • time between receiving e-mails and replying to them • number of great friends • number of new friends • number of offensive remarks • delivery reliability of my services • satisfaction score of my colleagues and employees • time spend with real friends • time spend at home with my children • number of times going out with children • number of times that my children involve me in their decisions regarding their lives • level of appreciation by colleagues • percent of my personnel who feel they have challenging work • percent of my customers who want to quit because of dissatisfaction • percent of completed, on-time deliveries, according to specifications • time needed to fix a complaint • percent of customers lost • number of visits to important customers • number of meetings with customer groups to be informed about their demands, requirements, ideas, and complaints • number of concrete objectives with regard to customer satisfaction • number of customer contacts • number of customer surveys • percent customer returns • percent customers satisfied with communication • degree of customer loyalty • costs associated with losing a customer or gaining a new customer • number of customer complaints regarding my behavior • number of concrete objectives with regard to customer satisfaction • perception score from others with regard to appreciation of the added value that I contribute
Knowledge & Learning	• number of personal core competencies • percent of learning objectives realized • percent of improvement actions achieved • number of time publicly sharing of knowledge • number of violin lessons • number of successful initiatives • number of management courses followed • percent of available management competencies

Table 2.2. Examples of Personal Performance Measures per BSC Perspective (Rampersad, 2005) (Cont.)

Perspective	*Personal Performance Measures*
	• percent of available strategic skills • number of new management books read • number of course days • number of workshops and seminars attended • number of required training courses • number of articles published • degree of client satisfaction with regard to my professionalism • number of study days • training costs • number of effective initiatives as a manager • number of effective initiatives implemented • number of conscious learning moments • sales based on newly acquired knowledge • number of speaking engagements • study expenditures • percent of taxable income for investment in personal development • ratio of number determined problems to solved problems • number of solved problems • number of suggestions implemented • number of innovative ideas which added value for others • time spend on reading, debating, discussing • number of books read about spirituality • number of successful strategic improvement proposals • number of innovative ideas • number of necessary skills • average time that I stay in the same position • percent of communication failures • lead time for product development • percent sales from new products • time needed to launch a new idea on the market (time-to-market) • experience level of my colleagues regarding knowledge exchange
Financial	• return stock investments • annual turnover own company • ratio earnings and expenses • level pension provisions • level of financial buffer • percent of deviation from the budget • percent of income from new orders • percent revenue from new products • balance savings account

Table 2.2. Examples of Personal Performance Measures per BSC Perspective (Rampersad, 2005) (Cont.)

Perspective	*Personal Performance Measures*
	• number of bills paid late • level of debt • savings balance • income growth • ratio of income to spending • earnings • salary • bonus level • cash flow • pension • disability insurance • investment level • profitability = sales ÷ costs + interests received • effectiveness = actual result ÷ expected result • labor productivity = result ÷ labor costs • labor costs = hours × hourly wage • daily rate as consultant • level of financial assets • percent of income for charities • number of successful acquisitions • level of household expenses • number of chargeable hours • number of unpaid "overhead" days own consulting firm • percent revenue from new products • time span between two paid consultancy orders • effectiveness = actual result ÷ expected result • operational costs as a percentage of sales • value added • value added per work time

Personal Targets

A personal target is a quantitative objective of a personal performance measure. It is a value that is pursued and then assessed through a personal performance measure. Targets indicate values that you want to achieve, and depend on your level of ambition. Performance measures and targets need to comply with SMART criteria, which means that they should be—

- *Specific*—They must be specifically formulated so that they can also influence behavior.

- *Measurable*—They must be formulated in such a way that they can measure the objective.
- *Achievable*—They must be realistic, realizable, feasible and acceptable.
- *Result-oriented*—They must be related to concrete results.
- *Time-specific*—They must be time-constrained.

Some examples of personal targets could be—increase of 15% over 2006, minimum 85% in two years, and maximum 92 kg as per December 31, 2006.

PERSONAL IMPROVEMENT ACTIONS

Personal improvement actions are strategies used to realize your personal ambition. They are utilized to develop your skills, improve your behavior, master yourself, and improve your performance. *How* is central here: How do I want to achieve my personal results? How can I realize my personal objectives? How can I improve my behavior? How can I ensure that I learn continuously, individually as well as collectively? How can I get to know myself better? How can I reduce my stress? The answer to the last question is that stress can be reduced by daily breathing and silence exercise, relaxation exercises, translating negative feelings into positive ones at every opportunity, creating enjoyment at work and in spare time, and increasing the experience of laughter. According to my family medical practitioner, the most important symptoms of stress are—a high level of sick leave, headaches, aggression, sleepless nights, nervousness, depression, high blood pressure, fatigue, fear, smoking and drinking heavily, lack of concentration, and memory loss. Deepak Chopra advises that exercise is an essential element in the process of creating inner harmony and a very effective way to battle stress and burnout and to improve sleep. He gives the following guidelines—

- Take daily walks of 30 minutes duration; the best time for this is from six to ten o'clock in the morning. Don't exercise after six o'clock at night, apart from quiet walks.
- You can also pick another kind of light to moderate uninterrupted exercise, such as cycling or swimming. A workout machine is suitable, too. Wear easy, loose-fitting clothes while exercising.
- Don't exercise right after you've eaten; wait for two to three hours.
- During exercises hold every pose for a short time and then release it gently. Focus your attention and breathing on the part of your body that is being stretched.
- Use only 50% of your physical capacity—if you are able to cycle about six miles, instead, cycle only three miles. By exercising regularly your ability will increase. Do not force your body.

- Do not exert yourself too much; during and after exercise you should feel energetic and strong, not fatigued and weak.
- If you are accustomed to exerting yourself a lot, reduce this to half during one month and see what this does for your sleep.

Exercise is necessary because in a sound body rests a sound mind. There is a strong mind–body connection; when the body is supple, free from tension, the mind is clear, calm and focused. This is why yoga is such a beneficial activity. It keeps the body relaxed so that the mind can follow. Almost anyone can reach the top, even people who were traumatized in their youth—like Thomas Edison, a sickly child, who was considered mentally challenged by his teacher; Eleanor Roosevelt, who was considered a lonely, neurotic girl; and Albert Einstein, whose early years were marked with fear and disappointment. All these people have left a great mark on the world. As Eleanor Roosevelt said—*"We gain strength, and courage, and confidence by each experience in which we really stop to look fear in the face ... we must do that which we think we cannot."*

Remember also what Martin Luther King, Jr. said—*"Put yourself in a state of mind where you say to yourself, 'Here is an opportunity for me to celebrate like never before, my own power, my own ability to get myself to do whatever is necessary'."*

PRACTICAL CASE: THE PERSONAL BALANCED SCORECARD OF JACK JOHNSON

Master your thoughts and you master your mind; master your mind and you master your life; master your life and you master your destiny.

—Robin Sharma

To illustrate what has been said about personal improvement actions, the personal ambition of Jack Johnson is shown in the box given here. He is the owner and CEO of a small management consulting firm in the UK, and a workaholic. He received complaints from customers frequently because of his rude behaviour and poor performance. His wife and children were also not quite happy with Jack because of the lack of balance between work and private life. Table 2.3 shows his most important critical success factors which are related to his personal ambition. These are factors which make him unique and in which he will further develop and distinguish himself. These factors have been identified in his personal ambition and in his PBSC are further developed (see Table 2.4). Work and spare time are explicitly included.

Personal Ambition of Jack Johnson

Personal Mission

Enjoy the freedom to serve others and to create a world of love and empowerment.

Personal Vision

I want to fulfill my mission in the following way:

- Earn the respect of my customers, colleagues, friends and loved ones
- Continue to look for challenges in my work, accept them and enjoy doing so
- Help organizations to be successful
- Continue to further develop my skills and competencies, and learn continuously
- Not act in conflict with my conscience
- Continue to increase my inner strength and keep this in balance with my physical health
- Achieve financial security

Personal Key Roles

In order to achieve my mission, the following key roles have top priority:

- *Spouse:* A maximum fulfillment of what is important for Karin, based on love, faithfulness, support and unconditional trust
- *Father:* Be an example for Frank and John so that they treat themselves and the people around them with respect and give them the ability to make the right choices and take decisions
- *Consultant:* Competent, honest, cooperative, and committed
- *Fellow man:* Give and receive trust

Table 2.3. Personal Critical Success Factors of Jack Johnson

Internal	*External*
• Continue look for challenges in my work, accept them and enjoy this • Not act in conflict with my conscience • Continue to increase my inner strength and keep it in balance with my physical health	• Enjoy the freedom to serve others and to create a world of love and empowerment. • Earn the respect of my customers, colleagues, friends and loved ones • Support organizations in being successful • Maximum fulfillment of what is important for Karin • Be an example for Frank and John • Give and receive trust
Knowledge & Learning	*Financial*
• Continue to increase my knowledge and skills and continue to learn • Competent, honest, co-operative, and committed	• Financial security

Table 2.4. Personal Balanced Scorecard of Jack Johnson

Personal Critical Success Factors	*Personal Objectives*	*Personal Performance Measures*	*Persoanl Targets*	*Personal Improvement Actions*
		Internal		
Continue to look for challenges in my work, accept them and enjoy this	Pleasure in my work	Level of feeling happy at work	> 80% of my time	Set aside 20 minutes every morning for personal development matters. Starting the day with a breathing and silence exercise.
		Level of laughing at work	At least 10 minutes each day	Revitalize my habit of laughter. Following a laughter therapy.
		Percent of mental absence	Decrease of mental absence with 75% based on a number of 10 non productive hours per week in the period 2005–2007	Implement my PBSC in concordance with the PDAC cycle.
	No stress	Level of stress	Decrease of at least 75% within 6 months	Learn to meditate and doing yoga effectively. Stretching exercises for 15 minutes a day. Balance the times of stress with times of pure relaxation and leisure.
Not act in conflict with my conscience	Be transparent	Number of times that I receive positive feedback regarding my ethical behavior	Increase of at least 20% per year	Regularly bring my PBSC up-to-date and bring in line with my behavior.

Table 2.4. Personal Balanced Scorecard of Jack Johnson (Cont.)

Personal Critical Success Factors	*Personal Objectives*	*Personal Performance Measures*	*Persoanl Targets*	*Personal Improvement Actions*
Continue to increase my inner strength and keep it in balance with my physical health	Emotionally strong	Number of hours of sleep	6 hours per day	Not endlessly continue activities but define a deadline and stick to it. Pay attention to the quality of sleep, not the quantity.
	Balance between my IQ, emotional intelligence and spiritual intelligence	Level of well-being	> 90% of the time I am awake	Control my emotions better. Improve my self-discipline. Think positively. Develop my skill of sitting quietly, enjoying the powerful silence for at least ten minutes a day.
		Level of feeling at ease and relaxed	Continuously	Develop my ability to focus for extended periods of time and to build up my concentration muscles.
	Be physically strong and fit	Weight	Per 1 December 2005 weight loss of at least 25 lbs. Current weight 185 lbs.	Continue current diet. Less candy. Wine in stead of beer. Healthy food (fruit/vegetables).
		Physical fitness	Decrease body fat of 47.4 % to 29.1 % per 1 December 2005. Fit score per 1 September 2005 of 27. Is 8 currently.	At least 4 times a year a 200 mi bicycle trip. Golf once a week. Cycle at least 3000 mi per year. 3 times a week exercises at home. Rejoin tennis club. Initiate a training roster. Purchase new running shoes. Cycle to work once a week.

Table 2.4. Personal Balanced Scorecard of Jack Johnson (Cont.)

Personal Critical Success Factors	*Personal Objectives*	*Personal Performance Measures*	*Persoanl Targets*	*Personal Improvement Actions*
External				
Enjoy the freedom to serve others and to create a world of love and empowerment.	Satisfaction	Degree of satisfaction of others with regard to my contribution to a better world	Satisfaction score of at least 80% within 2 years	Act more helpful without trying to gain profits from it. Have a more serviceable attitude towards others.
		Number of donations per year	Minimum 6 times per year	Further analyse every request for help and be able to say yes as well as no.
Earning the respect of my customers, colleagues, friends and loved ones	Obtain customer trust	Delivery reliability of my services	At least 95% within the agreed deadlines	Ask feedback from customers on the quality of services rendered and document this. I will show more respect for my customers. I will communicate more clearly with my customers. I will be more involved in the customer's situation. I will coach myself in recognizing customer's wishes and opportunities to bind customers. A timely follow up of customer's complaints and keep them informed on progress. Strive to increase customer satisfaction. Regularly organise customer enquiries. Analyse and register customer's behavior. Develop and implement guidelines for maximum customer satisfaction.

Table 2.4. Personal Balanced Scorecard of Jack Johnson (Cont.)

Personal Critical Success Factors	*Personal Objectives*	*Personal Performance Measures*	*Persoanl Targets*	*Personal Improvement Actions*
	Delighted customers	Number of innovative ideas, which create values for my customers	At least 4 per year	At least once a week a group brainstorm regarding the development of new products and services.
	Colleagues and co-workers who are inwardly involved with our organization	Percent of personnel turnover	To reduce by minimum 50% within one year.	Start voluntary ambition meeting, informal and on monthly basis.
		Percent of sick leave	Less than 2% in one year	Align our shared business ambition with staff ambitions
	Improved satisfaction level from my colleagues and co-workers about my behavior	Satisfaction score of colleagues and co-workers	Minimum 80% within one and a half year	Listen better to my colleagues and employees, learn to be less arrogant and to respect them.
	Strong ties with great friends	Time spent with my best friends	Monthly contact	See, speak or write to good friends at least once a month. An early morning fishing trip with Fred.
		Number of new friends	At least one per week	Make new friends and keep an updated list of all contacts.
	More spare time with my family	Total leave days	Minimum twenty per year	Go on vacation three times a year with my family.
	Be a good father	Time spent with the children	At least 1 hour per day	Do more together with the children. Have a more proactive approach towards the children. To share my PBSC with my children; decide to help them in formulating their own. To stimulate them to do breathing and silence exercise.

Table 2.4. Personal Balanced Scorecard of Jack Johnson (Cont.)

Personal Critical Success Factors	*Personal Objectives*	*Personal Performance Measures*	*Persoanl Targets*	*Personal Improvement Actions*
Be an example for Frank and John	Appreciation from Frank and John	Number of family outings	At least 2 times per month	Take the initiative to undertake something together.
		Number of times that Frank and John involve me in their decisions	Whenever needed	Show more patience to Frank and John; to listen more to them more carefully. Take an interested position, not a correcting one. Periodically inform, coach, advise and facilitate.
Maximum fulfillment of what is important for Karin	Be a good husband	Number of good conversations with Karin	At least one every day	Share all challenges, problems, ideas, successes with Karin. Share my PBSC with Karin; assist her in formulating her own. To breathe in more life in our relationship on this basis; Do the breathing and silence exercise together. A romantic picnic in the country every month.
	Caring and loving relationship with Karin	Number of loving and appreciating feedback received from Karin	Minimum of once per day	Make loving remarks self. Be open for her real needs. Take a subscription on theatre visits.
Support organizations in being successful	Be of additional value to organizations	Number of succour consultancy projects	Minimum annual increase of 10%	Develop knowledge in the areas of financial and HR management.
Give and receive trust	Add value to the life of others	Level of satisfaction of others regarding my actions	Increase of 20% within 1 year	Make a weekly balance to be reported in my silence book. To do more positive things for others.

Table 2.4. Personal Balanced Scorecard of Jack Johnson (Cont.)

Personal Critical Success Factors	*Personal Objectives*	*Personal Performance Measures*	*Persoanl Targets*	*Personal Improvement Actions*
		Knowledge & Learning		
Continue increase my knowledge and skills and continue to learn	MBA Graduate	MBA graduation	Graduation December 2007	Make study plans within 3 months. Start with graduation paper on 1/5/2007.
	Pro-active and action-directed advisor	Number of successful strategic improvement proposals to help serve our customers better.	At least one a week	Structure creative thinking process and aims, brainstorming, mind mapping. Organize a relaxation mid-week more initiative and be more decisive. More proactive, more effective, more result focussed and act with more persuasion.
	Professional and creative	Customer satisfaction related to my professionalism	Average 85% per November 2007	Apply brainstorming and mind mapping more often and more systematically.
		Number of study days	10–15 per year	Consider my PBSC as a living document and implement this in accordance with the PDAC-cycle.
		Number of hours per year to learn effectively	At least 400	Plan studies and measure progress. Learning by doing. Daring to do things in order to further develop my self-confidence.
	Improved leadership skills	Percent of personnel who find they are working under effective leadership	85% within 1 year	Subscribe to a conflict solving and corporate ethics course. Expand communicative competencies. Remain honest towards myself, and others. Develop my coaching skills. Speak more slowly.

Table 2.4. Personal Balanced Scorecard of Jack Johnson (Cont.)

Personal Critical Success Factors	*Personal Objectives*	*Personal Performance Measures*	*Persoanl Targets*	*Personal Improvement Actions*
Competent, honest, cooperative, and committed	Successful and professional consultant	Number of successful consultancy projects	At least 8 per year	Be able to confidently address a group without apprehension. Self-study PowerPoint before the end of 2007. Improve my listening skills. Setting up and implementing the TPS Code of Ethics in our service and on our site. Including business ethics in our service parcel. Considering the Total Performance Scorecard the guideline to our way of life.
		Number of implemented effective initiatives as a consultant	Minimum increase of 30% per year	
		Number of learning moments	At least 1 per week	Maintain a "learning moment" journal. Exchange experience and share knowledge with others.
		Financial		
Financial securities	Improved asset management	ROI stock portfolio	8 % per year	Pursue proven investment strategies
	Financially healthy	Turnover own consulting firm	Minimum of $850,000 per year as from 2007 (my own income minimum $150,000 per year).	Formulate the OBSC of our organization. Develop my acquisition skills. Learn to better use them.
	Financial stability for the future	Pension provisions	A pension of $3,000 per month minimum from my 65th year	Arrange pension insurance.

Table 2.4. Personal Balanced Scorecard of Jack Johnson (Cont.)

Personal Critical Success Factors	*Personal Objectives*	*Personal Performance Measures*	*Persoanl Targets*	*Personal Improvement Actions*
		Disability insurance	A minimum income of $3,000 per month in the case of disability	Arrange disability insurance.
	No financial problems	Level and quality of my financial reserves	Reserve of minimum 1 year	Continuously obtain new assignments for my consultancy. Exercise more initiatives. Develop and launch two new products per year.
	Continuity of assignments via own consultancy	Period between two assignments	Maximum 1 month	More sales discussions. Decisive action regarding sales activities. Develop Brochure and other PR-materials before 1/10/2007. Publish two articles latest 1/9/2005. Create website latest 1/8/2008. Act more pro-actively by being attentive of trends and developments. Prioritise appropriately. 3 Acquisition appointments per week. Improved networking and increased frequency of visits to networking occasions.
	Manage expenditures	Income and expense ratio	Increase of minimum 5% per year	Maintain a monthly budget

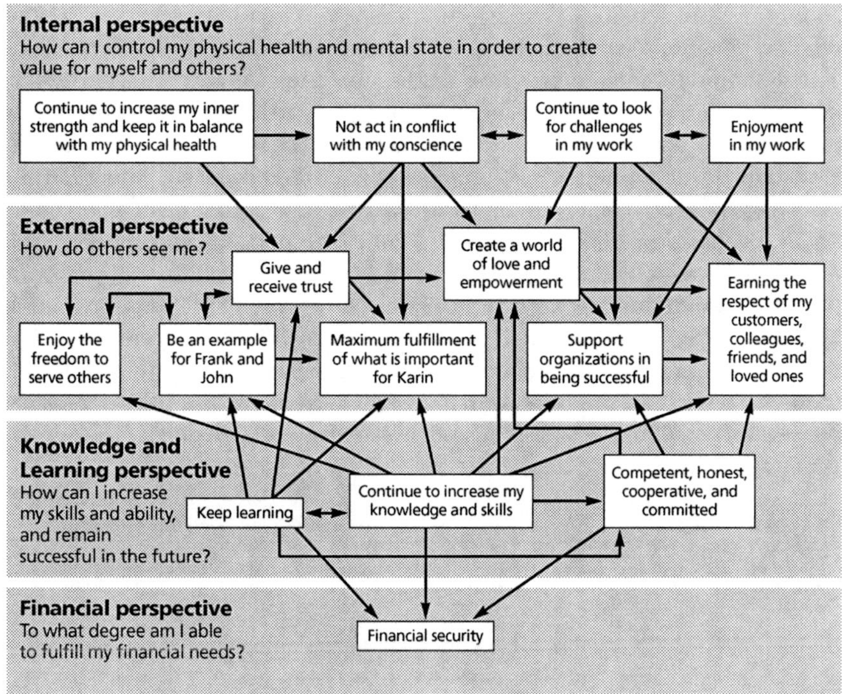

Figure 2.7. Relationships between Personal Critical Success Factors of Jack Johnson

Figure 2.7 shows the relationship between the critical success factors of Jack Johnson. On the basis of this diagram, you will be able to gain more insight into yourself. It is also a handy tool in communicating your PBSC to your trusted person. A trusted person is somebody who you trust, who respects you, who will guide you, who gives you feedback, who has consideration for you, is a mentor with your best interests in mind and offers you good guidance based on your PBSC.

CAUSE-AND-EFFECT RELATIONSHIP

There are seven sins in the world: Wealth without work, Pleasure without conscience, Knowledge without character, Commerce without morality, Science without humanity, Worship without sacrifice and Politics without principle.

—Mahatma Gandhi

All personal objectives should be interrelated and should affect one another. An objective is used to achieve another objective, which will result in the final objective. The final objective of many people is *to be happy*. This has to do with the meaning of life, that is, survival, comfort and enjoyment. It is an area about which we can do something; we should prepare for and cultivate it. The relation between several objectives is clearly conveyed in a cause effect chain. The position of these objectives, within the four perspectives, and their mutual relations are made visible in Figure 2.8. Include only the objectives that lead to the final objective. The cause-effect chain is a handy resource, enabling you to get better insight and to better communicate your PBSC to your trusted person, who, on its basis, will give you honest feedback. Figure 2.8 shows the cause-effect chain in relation to the personal objectives of Jack Johnson. All formulated objectives which lead to satisfaction, enjoyment in your work, emotional strength and balance between IQ, EQ (emotional intelligence, and SQ (spiritual intelligence) are displayed. Their positions within the four perspectives and their mutual relationships are clearly visible. All these goals result in the final overall objective (personal mission)—*"enjoy the freedom to serve others and to create a world of love and empowerment."*

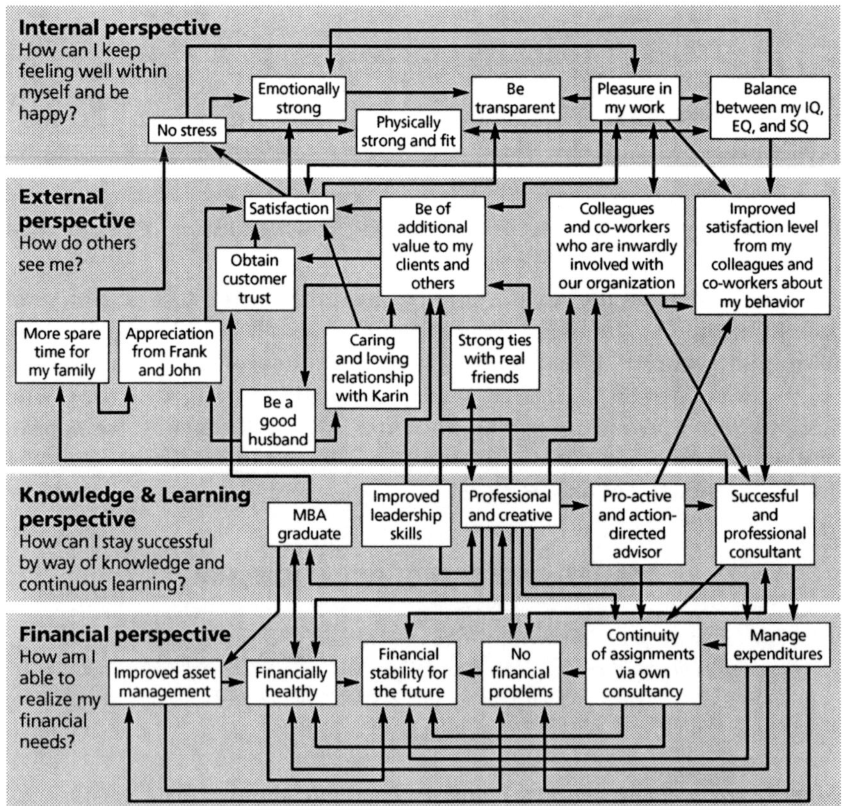

Figure 2.8. Cause-and-Effect Chain Regarding the Personal Objectives of Jack Johnson

GIVING PRIORITY TO PERSONAL IMPROVEMENT ACTIONS

When you cannot make up your mind which of two evenly balanced courses of action you should take—choose the bolder.

—W. J. Slim

Because there are many possible improvement actions, it is recommended to make a selection through prioritizing. After all, dedication to an improvement action is much easier when the choice is clear. There are various ways to assign a priority number to the improvement actions. Here, I introduce an integral method which has proven itself in practice. In this approach, those personal improvement actions which contribute the greatest to the most important personal critical success factors (CSFs) receive the highest priority. The score for each improvement action is determined as follows (Rampersad, 2003):

- Giving a weight (W1) to the critical success factor in question.
- Giving a weight (W2) to the contribution of the improvement action in question to the critical success factor.
- Multiplying these two weights to obtain the priority score (formula: $P = W1 \times W2$).

Table 2.5. W1 and W2 Factors

The W1 factors are determined using the following scale:	*The W2 factors were scaled as follows:*
1 = unimportant	1 = no contribution
2 = somewhat unimportant	2 = hardly any contribution
3 = less important	3 = average contribution
4 = important	4 = high contribution
5 = very important	5 = very high contribution

The weights W1 and W2 are first estimated based on a number between one and five (see Table 2.5). The more important the personal CSF, the higher would be the value of the W1 factor. Similarly, the higher the contribution of the personal improvement action to the CSF, the higher would be the W2 factor. The factor P is calculated by multiplying both average weights. Improvement actions with the highest P-factor (for instance ≥ 20) are part of the pre-selection. Then, the following criteria must be taken into consideration for the final selection of improvement actions—

- Time needed for the implementation of the improvement action and the realization of the related personal objective
- Costs related to the improvement action

- The global costs-benefits ratio
- The chances of the improvement action being successful (both manageable and realizable)
- It is best to start with a simple objective and the corresponding improvement actions, keeping in mind the above-mentioned aspects. Afterwards, bigger challenges can be taken on by selecting a corresponding improvement action and get going with it (see next chapter).

To illustrate this selection procedure, the priority number for each of Jack Johnson's personal improvement actions in relation to the knowledge and learning perspective is displayed in Table 2.6.

It is shown that the following improvement actions were preselected by Jack—

- "Take more initiative and be more decisive, proactive, effective, result focused and act with more persuasion"
- "Consider my PBSC a living document and implement this in accordance with the PDAC cycle"
- "Develop my coaching skills"
- "Remain honest towards myself and others"
- "Improve my listening skills," and
- "Maintain a learning moment journal."

All of these have a P-factor ≥ 20. In the next chapter I will focus on the implementation of the PBSC in accordance with the PDAC cycle.

Table 2.6. Priority Number of Each Personal Improvement of Jack Johnson, Regarding the Knowledge and Learning Perspective

Personal Improvement Actions	*Contribution to Personal Critical Success Factor*	*Weight Personal Critical Success Factor*	*Contribution of Personal Improvement Action to Critical Success Factor*	*Priority Number of Personal Improvement Actions*
		W1	*W2*	*P = W1 × W2*
Make study plans within 3 months	Continue increase my knowledge and skills and continue to learn	4	4	16
Start with graduation paper on 1/5/2007			3	12
Structure creative thinking process and aims, brainstorming, mind mapping			3	12
Organize a relaxation midweek once a year to obtain fresh inspiration			3	12

Table 2.6. Priority Number of Each Personal Improvement of Jack Johnson, Regarding the Knowledge and Learning Perspective

Personal Improvement Actions	*Contribution to Personal Critical Success Factor*	*Weight Personal Critical Success Factor* *W1*	*Contribution of Personal Improvement Action to Critical Success Factor* *W2*	*Priority Number of Personal Improvement Actions* *P = W1 × W2*
Take more initiative and be more decisive. More proactive, more effective, more result focussed and act with more persuasion			5	20
Apply brainstorming and mind mapping more often and systematically			4	16
Consider my PBSC as a living document and implement this in accordance with the PDAC-cycle			5	20
Plan studies and measure progress			3	12
Learning by doing. Daring to do things in order to further develop my self-confidence			4	16
Subscribe to a conflict solving and corporate ethics course			2	8
Expand my communicative competencies			3	12
Remain honest towards myself and others			5	20
Develop my coaching skills			5	20
Speak more slowly			4	16
Be able to confidently address a group without apprehension	Competent, honest, cooperative, and committed	5	3	15
Self-study PowerPoint before the end of 2007			1	5
Improve my listening skills			4	20

Table 2.6. Priority Number of Each Personal Improvement of Jack Johnson, Regarding the Knowledge and Learning Perspective

Personal Improvement Actions	*Contribution to Personal Critical Success Factor*	*Weight Personal Critical Success Factor*	*Contribution of Personal Improvement Action to Critical Success Factor*	*Priority Number of Personal Improvement Actions*
		W1	*W2*	*P = W1 × W2*
Setting up and implementing the TPS Code of Ethics in our service and on our site. Including business ethics in our service parcel. Considering the Total Performance Scorecard the guideline to our way of life.			3	15
Maintain a learning moment journal			5	25
Exchange experience and share knowledge with others			2	10

CHAPTER 3

IMPLEMENTING THE PERSONAL BALANCED SCORECARD

There is a direct correspondence between man's inner life of thoughts, feelings and impulses—his consciousness—and the circumstances and events in this outer environment. The external situation is an extension of his inner consciousness expressed in outer life.... Man's ego acts as a knot dividing the individual from the world around, the inner from the outer.... The higher, less selfish, personal and egoistic one's motivation, the more he grows, and the more he receives.

—Gary Jacobs

The next step in the personal coaching and self-development process is the implementation of the Personal Balanced Scorecard (PBSC) you have formulated. This is necessary to let your awareness grow gradually, to continuously develop your skills and to become more creative on the basis of the PBSC. I introduce a new learning cycle to accomplish this, the Plan-Do-Act-Challenge cycle (PDAC cycle), which is followed continuously (see Figure 3.1). To live in accordance with the PBSC through its implementation using the PDAC cycle results in cyclical learning and in a step-by-step process through which happiness, awareness, enjoyment, fun and creativity, at work as well in your spare time are increased. After all, when people are in control of their own actions and are free to face challenges, they tend to be

Personal Balanced Scorecard, pages 73–80

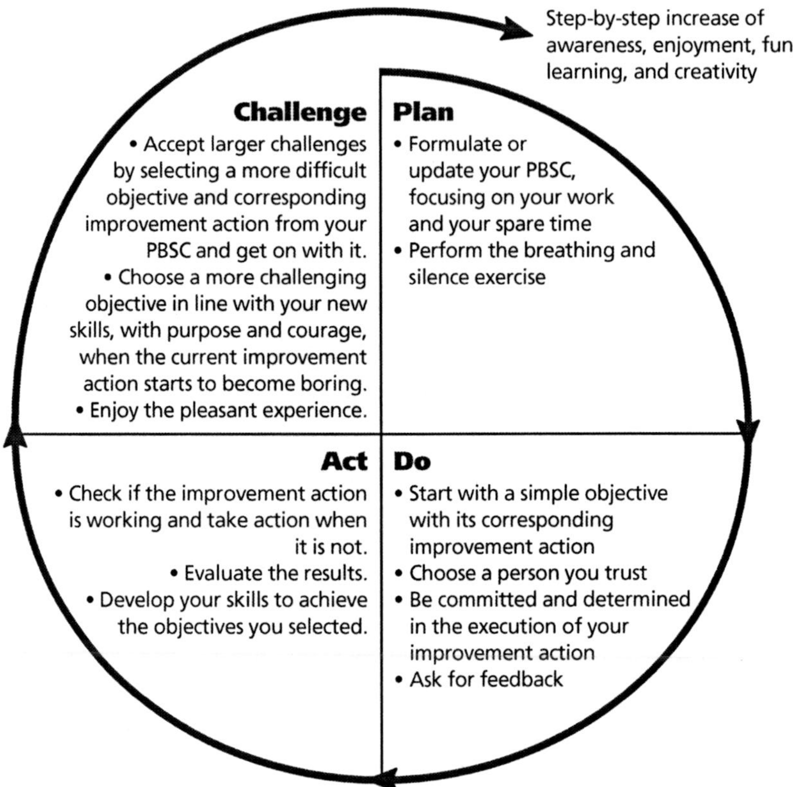

Figure 3.1. The PDAC Cycle (© Hubert Rampersad)

happier. The PDAC-cycle consists of the following four phases (Rampersad, 2005).

Plan—Formulate or update your PBSC, which focuses on your work as well as on your free time. Before you begin, use the breathing and silence exercise introduced earlier to achieve this. This exercise gives you more energy, which you need in order to transform your personal ambition into action (through personal objectives, performance measures and targets) with purpose and resolution.

Do—Start with a simple objective from your PBSC and the corresponding improvement action, keeping in mind the priorities that have been identified. Each morning when you rise, use the breathing and silence exercise, focus on a selected improvement action which you should then strive to implement during the day. Execute the improvement action with dedication, self-confidence, willpower and concentration. This must be in concordance with your present skills. Submit yourself

with courage to the related objective, even when you run into resistance. Be determined in the realization of your personal objectives and don't give up. Share your good intentions with a trusted person (spouse, friend, colleague or manager), who will ask questions, discuss with you, and give you honest feedback. Doing entails acting with purpose and making efforts to realize your objective. Ask for feedback often from the trusted person. This gives you the opportunity to measure what progress you have made. Start with habits which restrict you, influence your life unfavorably, and deliver poor results.
Act—Review the results according to the personal performance measures and targets you have defined earlier, measure your progress, and check to what extent you have realized your personal objectives. Check if the improvement action is working, and take action if it is not. If you have not been able to realize your objective, please do not worry about it. Just start again. You will improve steadily. It becomes a habit to do things right the first time if you evaluate your PBSC each month with your trusted person, and learn from experience. Think of three people, who can act as your trusted person; who give you inspiration and motivation for the realization of your objectives and improvement actions. Plan to meet with each one of them regularly. Listen enthusiastically to them, brainstorm with them, and take their counsel. Develop your skills and competencies to achieve the objectives you have selected. Recognize your responsibility to constantly develop yourself. Implement the personal improvements, assess the personal results, document the lessons learned, and improve and monitor your actions and thinking continuously. Also think about bringing your personal ambition and your personal behavior in balance, which will influence your ethical behavior. After a few weeks, you will notice small differences in yourself. In two months, the behavioral change will become firmly embedded. After five months, the important personal quality you desired will be yours. Also in this stage you should use the breathing and silence exercise.
Challenge—Accept bigger challenges by selecting a more difficult objective and the corresponding improvement action from your PBSC and act on it. Be conscientious in choosing a more challenging objective on par with your improved skills when the current improvement action starts becoming boring. Enjoy the experience and document what you have learned and unlearned during the execution of the improvement action. Refine it and review your PBSC regularly.

In summary, it boils down to this—formulate your long-term personal ambition and short-term SMART objectives with corresponding improvement actions, perform the breathing and silence exercise regularly, aim your spiritual energy at your improvement action, chose a trusted person, get going with your improvement action with dedication and resolution, request feedback and pay attention that the improvement action and the new challenge correspond with your skills. Since the PDAC cycle keeps on running through this, you create a stable basis for maximum individual development and personal well being. Through this, you can work passionately toward inner and outer excellence, can decide your own fate and can become more self-confident. You will also create a feeling of inner security. You will become a better person on the basis of the match between personal ambition and personal behavior, in combination with practice of the breathing and silence exercise. Implementation of your PBSC in accordance with the PDAC cycle results in a process of total involvement with life, and it will make you feel content with the challenging activity so that you will forget everything around you. This process is called *Flow* by the well-known Hungarian-American psychologist, Mihaly Csikszentmihalyi (1990). Flow is the result of a conscious effort to conquer a challenge; it is the result of a search for optimum experiences, the constant discovery of new challenges and the continuous development of new skills. According to Csikszentmihalyi, someone is in flow when both challenges and skills are at a high level. People feel happier, more cheerful, stronger, more active, more creative and satisfied in this situation. It has been hypothesized that happy people may be healthier both mentally and physically than less happy people.

Consider Robin Sharma's ten fundamentals of happiness—

- Pursue a productive, exciting and active life
- Engage in meaningful activities every minute of every day
- Develop an organized, planned lifestyle with little chaos
- Set realistic goals yet keep your mark high
- Think positively—you cannot afford the luxury of a negative thought
- Avoid needless worry over trifling matters
- Devote time to fun
- Develop a warm, outgoing personality with a sincere love for people
- Get in the habit of giving more than receiving
- Learn to live in the present. The past is water under the bridge of life.

He advises the following actions to enhance personal effectiveness

> Spend ten minutes every night before you go to bed in self-examination. Think about the good things you did during the day and the bad actions you may have taken which you must change in order to excel and grow. Successful people are simply more thoughtful than others. Daily reflection will soon allow for the eradication of your negative qualities and will sharpen the mind. After steady practice, a time will eventually arrive when the mistakes you make are few indeed and your personal power will move to the highest level.

Application of the PBSC method and implementation in accordance with the PDAC cycle produces flow. You will expand your individual awareness to universal awareness and will master yourself. It will open up new horizons for you in your quest for an optimal state of health and happiness. By applying the PBSC to your family, you can realize your family objectives and improve relations with your loved ones.

Formulating and implementation of your personal ambition in accordance with the PDAC cycle, also results in managing your intuition effectively. Weston Agor on this says

> Tomorrow's managers will face extremely complex situations in which they will need to make decisions under circumstances where the complete data necessary for traditional decision-making process will be unavailable, inadequate, or too costly to gather quickly. They will be dealing with a changing world and a work-force that will make increasing demands for real participation in the decision-making process. Managers will need to rely less on formal authority and more on intuitive judgment in order to handle the shift to bottom-up, horizontal organizational communication with sensibility and persuasiveness. Managers will need a new set of skills to cope with this shifting environment. Until now, the predominant management approach has been the logical, analytical, left-brain style.... Intuition will become more and more valuable during the coming period of surprises, complexities, and rapid changes. Intuition becomes more efficient as we become more open to our feelings and more secure trough experience in its ability to provide the correct cues. The first rule is to believe in it. The second rule is practice makes perfect. With effort and persistence, we can develop our intuition. The third rule is to create a supportive environment in which intuitive skills are valued.

The boxed text below shows some activities related to ongoing personal improvement in accordance with the PBSC (see also Chapter 9).

Activities Related to Continuous Personal Improvement in Accordance with the PBSC (Rampersad, 2005)

- Formulate and study your PBSC and evaluate it regularly.
- Evaluate the necessity of personal growth and educate yourself continuously. According to Einstein: "Education is what remains after one has forgotten what one has learned in school".
- Constantly engage in new challenges and develop related skills.
- Perform the breathing and silence exercise every morning for about 20 minutes. This may later be expanded to 40-50 minutes a day. The breathing exercise gives you more energy and reduces stress, which is needed to transform your personal ambition with purpose and resolution into action.

- Share the work-related elements of your PBSC with your manager also.
- Implement your PBSC routinely on the basis of the PDAC cycle. Act with purpose and make efforts to realize your ambition.
- Ask your manager, colleagues, co-workers, clients and others whom you trust for feedback. Ask them for comments and impressions with regard to your actions. Regularly analyze your relationship with them.
- Also focus on things which are not your strong points; the habits which curtail you and have a negative influence on your life, as well as bring bad results.
- Evaluate the results of the PBSC implementation. Compare these with the personal performance measures and objectives in your PBSC.
- Check if you have realized your personal objectives.
- Adjust your PBSC continuously. It is a living document.
- Evaluate your ethical behavior constantly on the basis of your PBSC.
- Make time in your schedule to improve yourself continuously and to assist others in improving themselves.
- Develop your intuitive skills on the basis of your PBSC. To make decisions on the basis of intuition is to be quick, accurate and effective.
- Be unselfish and serve others. Use your talents to serve mankind. Do not live for yourself, but for the world. The more you give, the more you will receive. Learn to give what you would like to have. Ask not what this world can do for you, but, rather, what you can do for this world. Make service an important goal in your life. Be the person who is always concerned about others.
- Do not waste energy on your ego. Mahatma Gandhi once said that the ego should be at zero to be able to find freedom.
- Recognize your responsibility and ethical duty to constantly improve and develop yourself in the interests of yourself, your loved ones, your job, your organization and your society.
- Think of continuous learning in accordance with the PDAC cycle as a challenge and with this increase your creativity.
- Constantly evaluate in order to make decisions based on facts.
- Use the PBSC in combination with the breathing and silence exercise to develop your awareness, to create inner peace, to be innovative and to generate new ideas.
- Maintain a positive attitude toward life, remain calm, controlled and critically evaluate your behavior.
- Trust in your ability to learn and believe in yourself. Firmly believe in what you want. Norman Vincent Peale said: "Believe in yourself! Have faith in your abilities! Without a humble but reasonable confidence in your own powers you cannot be successful or happy." Remember also what Gandhi said: "To believe in something, and not to live it, is dishonest."
- Respect others, speak honestly and positively about them and judge them objectively.

- Pay attention to your spiritual development in order to reach a higher level of self-consciousness.
- Coach yourself on the basis of your PBSC and PDAC cycle and live in harmony with your formulated personal ambition.
- Match your personal ambition with your personal ethical behavior, in order not to act in conflict with your conscience, and thus influence your ethical behavior favorably. Try to become a better human being.
- Match your personal ambition with the shared ambition to be able to work with pleasure and to be intrinsically involved in your work without facing stress and burnout.
- Communicate with your manager by way of an informal and voluntary ambition meeting. Take the initiative yourself. Ask your manager to formulate his/her PBSC too and to share it with you. This will bring about an atmosphere of mutual trust.
- Document the learned and unlearned lessons regularly.
- Make a routine of personal improvement.
- Do not strive for success, but for perfection.
- Celebrate your successes and enjoy the optimum experiences you acquire through this way of life.
- Grab your chance and take on greater challenges often by again and again selecting a more difficult objective with corresponding improvement action from your PBSC, and to get on with it. Learning will become a pleasure, which will allow you to improve continuously.
- Apply the PBSC method and PDAC cycle also to your family life, to enable you to realize family objectives and to breathe new life in your relationships with loved ones. Assist family members to formulate their PBSCs and have them share it with each other. After all, one who cannot function well in his/her family cannot function well at work, either.
- Apply the PBSC method and PDAC cycle at school as well in order to study better and faster.

The boxed text below shows some important steps in the PBSC process.

Ten Steps in the PBSC Coaching Process

1. Look for a quiet spot and perform the workshop's breathing and silence exercise to reflect on the personal ambition questions.
2. Choose an experienced coach (preferable PBSC trained coach) to help you in this process and allow this person to ask/discuss the ambition questions leading to your personal ambition statement (mission, vision and key roles).
3. Draft a statement of your personal mission and vision. Make sure that all four PBSC perspectives (internal, external, knowledge/learning, and financial) are included.

4. Formulate your related personal key roles.
5. Write these down again with the help of your coach. You can make a selection of ambition questions from the PBSC book.
6. Identify and select your critical success factors within your personal ambition statement and translate these into personal objectives with corresponding measures, targets, and improvement actions. Take into account the four PBSC perspectives: internal, external, knowledge/learning, and financial.
7. Improve yourself continuously by implementing your PBSC according to the Plan-Do-Act-Challenge cycle. Get going with your improvement actions with dedication and resolution. Meet with your coach and request feedback. Meet with him/her regularly, listen to him/her, and take his/her counsel. Reflect and update your PBSC from time to time, it's a living document.
8. Develop inner peace and personal integrity by aligning your personal ambition with your behavior in order to develop your personal integrity. This self-awareness process is based on integrity questions from the workshop. This process of self-assessment will cause a deeper connection to your self.
9. Alignment of your personal ambitions with the shared organizational ambitions, through use of an Ambition Meeting between you and your line manager. This provokes commitment, inner and outer involvement, and motivation. The ambition meeting is a periodic, informal, voluntary and confidential meeting between line-manager and his/her employees. The line-manager can make a selection of ambition questions (see book), which he/she can use during the ambition meeting.
10. Coach the line manager to coach his/her employees based on the PBSC system to form a solid, trusted, coaching relationship.

CHAPTER 4

ALIGNING PERSONAL AMBITION WITH PERSONAL BEHAVIOR, PERSONAL INTEGRITY

It has become dramatically clear that the foundation of corporate integrity is personal integrity.

—Sam DiPiazza, CEO of PricewaterhouseCoopers

The balance between personal ambition and ethical behavior is the next step towards lasting personal growth and reinforcing honesty and trustworthiness. The time is ripe for a new basis of ethical and spiritual leadership based on personal integrity. I am referring to Miller and Pruzan (2003)—*"There is such a need for a complete rebirth of trust in our business leaders. Somewhere along the line leaders lost their humility and in doing so they have lost their compassion and empathy, and their inner connection to God."*

Formulating your PBSC, implementing this in accordance with the PDAC-cycle and finding the proper balance between your personal ambition and your behavior results in inner peace and the ability to be guided by your inner voice. All of this develops personal charisma, trust and personal integrity. People with this perspective on life matter to one another and create a stable basis for their own credibility. When people achieve this

Personal Balanced Scorecard, pages 81–86

inner authority, they also have a positive effect on the loyalty, motivation, and dedication of those around them. According to Kouzes and Posner, the credibility of people depends on the following—

- Trustworthy people practice what they preach; they suit the action to the word.
- They keep their word and promises.
- Their actions match their words; they do what they said they would do.

Indeed, while we judge ourselves by our invisible behavioral patterns, others judge us by our visible behavioral patterns—what we do and say. The balancing process spoken of is about the interaction between your aspirations, intentions, purpose, principles, ethical standards, and values—in other words, your personal ambition—and how others interpret you (your ethical behavior). There is always a potential difference (which is often difficult to accept) between how you see yourself (who you want to be), and how others see and judge you. To become the person envisioned in your personal ambition, you also have to know how others see you and what they think of you. When you know this, your self-knowledge increases and you are able to improve the effectiveness of your actions. Therefore, this process of developing self-knowledge involves the establishment of a balance between your personal ambition (which envisions a higher level of consciousness) and your personal behavior (which refers to your present behavior). (see Figure 4.1). As we have discussed, your personal ambition is also shaped by your mindset. Behind these opinions, your motives and inner needs which are expressed in your behavior are hidden. In order to achieve real personal improvement and growth, it is necessary first to find a balance between your personal behavior and your personal ambition:

Personal (<Mission>, <Vision>, <Key Roles>) » Personal behavior
Personal Ambition » Personal behavior

The central questions in this contemplative process are:

- Do I act in accordance with my conscience?
- Is there consistency between what I am thinking and what I am doing?
- How do my ideals, ambitions, intentions, needs, and deepest desires fit my present actions?
- Are my thoughts and my practices the same?
- Do I act in accordance with my personal ambition?
- Does my personal ambition reflect my desire to act ethically?
- Are there contradictions in my personal ambition?
- In what way does my behavior influence my views, and vice versa?

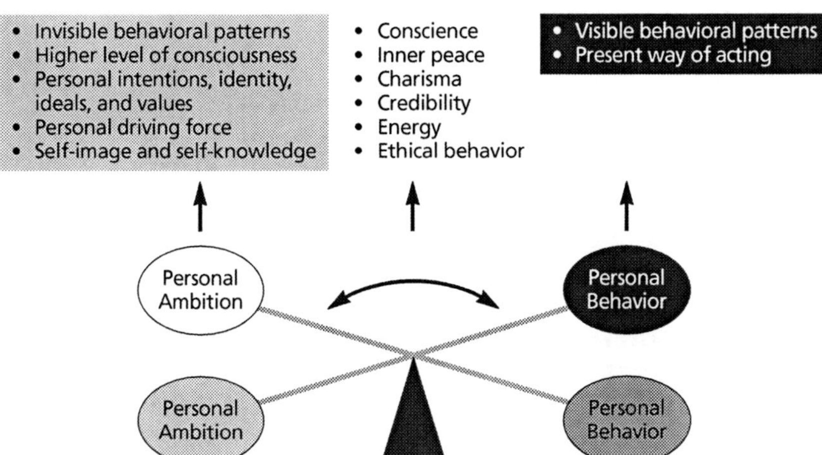

Figure 4.1. Aligning Personal Ambition with Personal Behavior

Your personal ambition and your practices must be the same. When people find harmony between their personal ambition and their personal behavior, they will not come into conflict with their conscience.

Then you can work authentically and purposefully at continuous personal improvement and development without wasting energy. Robin Sharma said—*"Be the master of your will but the servant of your conscience."*

According to Selvazajan Yesudian, our conscience is the inner voice that talks to us with firm conviction to help us distinguish between right and wrong, between fact and fiction. It is a voice that whispers to us what we can do best and guides us in our daily activities. It is a voice that we can trust and on which we can build our existence. It is the only reliable compass to follow if there is a conflict between the mind that reasons and the heart that decides. Harmony between personal ambition and personal behavior ensures that your deeds are in accord with your conscience. You will gain better insight into your behavior, your strengths and weaknesses and your related personal objectives. Also, it can be noted that the personal ambition not only supports insight, but also reality. Harmony between personal ambition and personal behavior also has to do with attentiveness, namely, to continuously perceive what you do and be aware of the influence of your behavior on human beings, animals, plants and the environment. As this attentiveness develops, your ethical behavior will increase. The breathing and silence exercise previously introduced and reflection on the match between personal ambition and personal behavior will help to stimulate your attentiveness. You will also become a better human being.

How to Look at Success

The best way to look at success is to ask.

- Have I followed my conscience?
- Have I given my best effort?
- Have I done what was right?
- Have I learned from my effort?

FORMULA OF RIGHT PERSONAL ACTION

Aligning your personal ambition with your personal behaviour ensures that your actions in society are *right* and in accordance with your conscience. Thomas Huxley has said—*"Learn what is true in order to do what is right."*

I have defined right personal action as—

Right personal action = Being + PBSC + Doing +
Aligning personal ambition with personal behavior

According to Chatterjee, right action is one that flows from our being; being is the very spirit of action (doing). I am of the opinion that you also should have insight into yourself on the basis of your PBSC and that your behavior should be in balance with your personal ambition to be able to act right. 'Doing' is also of importance as you will develop your skills based on this and enter into new challenges constantly.

FORMULA OF SELF-KNOWLEDGE

To summarize Part I of this book, I introduce the formula for self-knowledge, which is the core of the PBSC concept. Self-knowledge is *implicit knowledge,* which is inside your head. The PBSC transforms this self-knowledge into *explicit knowledge,* whereby you are better able to develop and control your self-knowledge. Making the *implicit* knowledge *explicit* has a favorable influence on your creativity. I have defined self-knowledge as a function of three core elements: *Personal Ambition, Thinking, and Doing* (see Figure 4.2). Therefore, self-knowledge is a function of *personal ambition, thinking and doing.*

<Self-knowledge> = f (<Personal Ambition>, <Thinking>, <Doing>)

The function f specifies the relation between self-knowledge and personal ambition, thinking and doing. The personal ambition component is related to your awareness and consists of information about yourself. It is

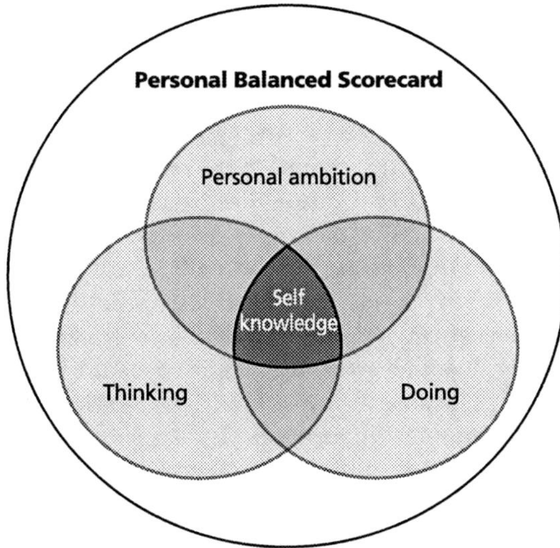

Figure 4.2. Self-knowledge serves as the Binding Tie in the PBSC concept (Rampersad, 2005)

connected to your motives, values, norms, opinion, principles and attitudes, which are the basis of your behavior. Thinking is necessary to provide you this insight, to which end I have introduced the breathing and silence exercise. In fact, breathing and the ability to think have the same origin in the human brain. Thought control follows breath control and vice versa. On the basis of the breathing and silence exercise, you can turn your attention inward and gain control over your awareness. Silence comprises the sharpening and better understanding of your spirit and results in a calm state of mind, which leads to clear thinking. This thinking process helps you bring the left side of your brain in balance with the right side. Doing is necessary to develop your skills on the basis of experience, to learn from this and to constantly enter into new challenges. For this purpose I have introduced the Plan-Do-Act-Challenge cycle. Learning by doing is necessary, because your personal ambition does not only rely on insight about yourself, but also on reality and the feedback which you receive from others. Doing is therefore related to your capabilities, skills, and personal experiences; in other words, what you are able to do, know and understand. Remember what Thomas Jefferson said—*"Do you want to know who you are? Don't ask. Act! Action will delineate and define you."*

The importance of learning by doing is illustrated by these statistics—

- After *reading* something, 10% is remembered.
- After *hearing* something, 20% is remembered.

- After *seeing* something, 30% is remembered.
- After *seeing and hearing* something, 50% is remembered.
- After *doing* something yourself, 90% is remembered

Learning is an important element in the self-knowledge formula. To be effective, one has to keep on learning. Learning is a continuous personal transformation. It is a cyclic and cumulative process of actualizing your self-knowledge (adding new information to your knowledge repertory) in order to qualitatively improve your actions. It is a permanent change of self-knowledge as a result of repeated experiences. In the scope of increasing shifts of *lifetime employment* to lifetime *employability*, you must ensure that your self-knowledge is up-to-date. After all, one is more successful if one can learn quicker and is able to implement self-knowledge quicker. A person who does not learn continuously, and is unable to continually develop, mobilize, cultivate, evaluate, utilize and maintain his/her self-knowledge, will not be able to operate effectively in this ever more complex society.

In short, to achieve optimum learning, it is important that people have the opportunity to do things. Learning can be categorized as self-learning and shared learning (team learning or organizational learning). Self-learning, which I have discussed above, is the source of all learning. For this, insight into your personal ambition is indispensable. People who do not have this insight are poor learners. Without self-learning, shared learning cannot exist. With self-learning, employees learn separately and experience an individual behavioral change. With shared learning they learn together, with and from each other. When shared learning occurs the whole organization learns, and undergoes a shared behavioral change, or organizational change. This applies to knowledge as well—Self-knowledge needs to be cultivated first before you can acquire knowledge of the world or your company. It's therefore important to make self-knowledge your best friend. In the next part of this book, I will go into the application of the PBSC more closely as a tool for managing talents effectively within organizations and to create more enjoyment and inner involvement among employees at the workplace.

PART II

PBSC AS AN INSTRUMENT FOR ENJOYMENT AND EFFECTIVE TALENT DEVELOPMENT AT WORK

The top priority in business—as corporations become the most powerful institution on the planet—seems to be the re-education of leaders. How can we effectively help competitive, short-term-results-oriented business executives to transform their mindset, challenge their assumptions about the purpose of the corporations they lead, challenge their own purpose in life, raise their consciousness? How can we help them to develop a statesman/woman view of the world thus enabling them to position their companies—not in the "market"—but within society as a whole?

—Oscar Motomura, Founder and CEO of the Amana-Key Group

CHAPTER 5

ALIGNING PERSONAL AMBITION WITH SHARED AMBITION

The most important mission for a Japanese manager is to develop a healthy relationship with his employees, to create a family within the corporation, a feeling that employee and managers share the same fate.

—Akio Morita, former Chairman of Sony Corporation

In the first part of this book, individual personal development was central and aimed at personal growth in life. In the second part, I will be looking closer at the application of the PBSC as a tool for effective talent management and for the creation of employees' enjoyment and inner involvement at the workplace. Thus, Part I forms the starting point. In the previous chapter, the mutual alignment between personal ambition and personal behavior was shown to be central in order to stimulate ethical behavior and to develop inner peace, personal charisma, and one's credibility. In this chapter, the alignment of the personal ambition with the shared organizational ambition is central for the purposes of commitment, trust, inner involvement, stress and burnout reduction, stimulating enjoyment, active participation, motivation and empowerment of employees. It has to do with reaching a higher degree of compatibility between personal and organizational objectives and mutual value addition (as shown in Figure 5.1). It means—

Personal Balanced Scorecard, pages 89–110

Personal (<Mission>,<Vision>,<Key Roles>) » Organizational (<Mission>, <Vision>,<Core Values>)
Personal Ambition » Shared Ambition

People do not work with devotion or expend energy on something they do not believe in or agree with. Clarity and uniformity of personal and organizational values and principles are therefore essential for the active involvement of people. Research has shown that when an individual has some input regarding the shared ambition that affects his or her work, the person will be more supportive, motivated, and receptive towards organizational change. Doing work that is interesting, exciting and provides learning has become a key personal driver. Experience teaches us that identification with the organization is the most important motive for employees to dedicate themselves actively to the organizational objectives and to maximize their human resource potential. All people have different personal values and principles that we must try to understand and link to the values of the organization. Organizational development and improvements can only be of a permanent nature by doing so. The experience of applying the PBSC in the past two years has shown that most employees want to be content and happy at their workplace, that they really enjoy going to work, that they strive for a balance between work and life and that they want to give 100% to the organization. Many managers do not anticipate this. The fact that 75–80% of all

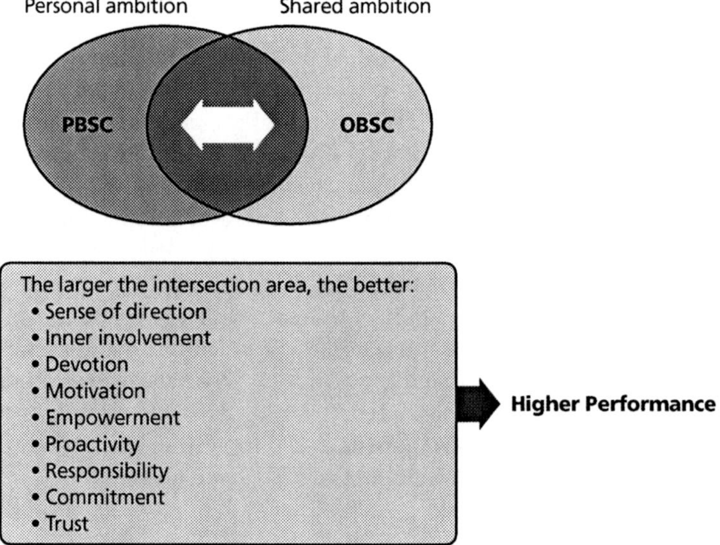

Figure 5.1. Match between Personal Ambition and Shared Ambition

organizational change and development projects in Europe has fail to do with the behavior and actions of managers which disrupt and frustrate the change process. This then combines with resistance to change and results in the creation of inability and incapability. Such behavior includes, for example—egotistic behavior, arrogance, immodesty, hidden agendas, lies, prioritizing own personal interests, ignoring staff, being bombastic, acting aimless, not showing respect, leaving employees to their fate, not paying attention to their development, poor listening, impatience, untrustworthiness, unreliability, not giving signs of appreciation, preferring communication through e-mail, being unapproachable, not showing drive, not keeping to high ethical norms and values, accentuating status differences, punishing employees who make mistakes, undermining and suppressing confidence of employees. U.S. workers have some serious qualms about their leaders, as The Globe and Mail newspaper commented (August 2005), with just 40 percent saying they trust top management to communicate honestly and only 38 percent saying leaders do a good job of explaining important business decisions, according to a survey of about 1,300 workers in more than 800 organizations in the United States by Mercer Human Resource Consulting. Less than half—49 percent—said their organizations, on the whole, are well-managed and the same percentage felt that senior management communicates a clear vision of the future direction of the organization, according to Mercer's 2005 What's Working survey.

It is time that managers unlearn the above-mentioned behaviors in the interests of the health and happiness of their employees. Public health scientists at University College London have found that people who have more moments of happiness over a day produce less harmful chemicals such as cortisol and so are likely to be healthier in the long run and less likely to suffer from heart disease. Managers instead of creating happiness create distrust and fear within the organization. They have an enormous destructive impact on the health of their people and their organization. As mentioned earlier, more than half of all employees in Europe have changed jobs or organizations at least once because of their manager's behavior—in other words, mismanagement is the reason for their poor performance on the job. True learning is not stimulated in an atmosphere of distrust and fear. This is an opportunity to create warmth, motivation, pleasure, passion, heartfelt commitment, and self-direction within companies, which is often missed. The result of such behaviors on the part of managers is that many organizations have to contend with mental absence, limited motivation, low labor productivity, lots of stress and burnout, individuals who are insufficiently result-oriented and action-driven, etc.

The concordance of personal ambition and shared organizational ambition should also take place at all levels of the organization. For this reason, it is important to know which specific inner needs are behind the behavior of the employees, and what motivates them to remain with the organization or leave it. The boxed text shows the results of research into the turnover factors for information technology personnel in The Netherlands and what their individual interests were (Wanrooy, 2001).

Turnover Factors for Information Technology Personnel in The Netherlands

Reasons to stay	*Reasons to leave*
1. In substance an interesting position, a lot of variation	1. Little or no challenges anymore
2. New challenges	2. In essence an uninteresting position
3. Steady job	3. Low income
4. More money	4. Little chance for promotion
5. Favorable place of business	5. Unpleasant colleagues
6. Promotion and career possibilities	6. Too much pressure at work
7. Independence	7. Little or no salary perspectives
8. Pleasant colleagues	8. Leader who does not stimulate
9. Income perspectives	9. Unfavorable place of business
10. Opportunities to follow training	10. Very little freedom

It is clear from this that new challenges and variety in the workplace are more important than salary for Dutch employees. Managers and their employees do not necessarily have similar perspectives on job-reward factors. Compared to employees, managers place greater importance on salary as a motivational tool. In January 2005, Sinead Finn, Sales and Marketing Manager Ryanair (the largest low cost airline in Europe, with 27.5 million passengers in 2004) stated in an interview—

> The most important for employees is the salary. We pay the highest average salary in the airline industry in Europe: on average over £50,000 per employee, Easyjet arrives at £42,000 and BA at £ 30,000 on average. This is the first and best stimulant.

At the same time, the ITF (International Transport Workers Federation) has launched a special website for Ryanair employees because there is so much fear in that organization since it recently forbade its employees to charge their personal cell phones at work (saving an estimated US$ 0.99 per employee per year). The text below outlines the differences between

Motivation: Employees versus Supervisors

A sample of industrial workers in the States was asked to rank ten "job-reward" factors. In addition, supervisors ranked the same factors, based on their perception of how workers would rank-order them.

Actual Worker Rankings	*Supervisor Perceptions of Worker Rankings*
1. Interesting work	1. Good wages
2. Full appreciation of work done	2. Job security
3. Feeling of being in on things	3. Promotion and growth in the organization
4. Job security	4. Good working conditions
5. Good wages	5. Interesting work
6. Promotion and growth in the organization	6. Personal loyalty to employees
7. Good working conditions	7. Tactful discipline
8. Personal loyalty to employees	8. Full appreciation of work done
9. Tactful discipline	9. Sympathetic help with personal problems
10. Sympathetic help with personal problems	10. Feeling of being in on things

the factors valued by U.S. employees and supervisors. Many factors valued by employees are non-monetary in nature (Kovach, 1987).

Management has two general options of rewards regarding motivation: extrinsic (such as salary, money) and intrinsic (for example, recognition, appreciation, and praise). Intrinsic motivation is that which is inherently pleasurable, while extrinsic motivation is not. Intrinsic motivators are those that arise from within—doing something because you enjoy it—while extrinsic motivators mean people are seeking a reward, such as money. Money has lost its impact on employee's motivation, as it is a short-term incentive. Therefore, organizations must reward employees intrinsically, too. A climate of learning, challenges, enjoyment, happiness, trust, creativity, self-actualization, self-development, esteem, and inner involvement is often more important to employees than salary. Stimulating the employees and making a job more enjoyable are the changes managers have to make in order to attract and engage workers, whose fundamental views about work have been shifting radically over the past ten years.

Bestselling psychologist Mihaly Csikszentmihalyi (1990) did large-scale research in the United States about dissatisfaction of employees. It was established that American employees named three important reasons why they were dissatisfied with their job. These reasons had to do with the quality of the experience on the job, and not with salary and other material interests. The first and most important reason was about the lack of variations and challenges (dull and senseless). The second reason was related to conflicts with other people at work, in particular with bosses. The conflict is often because of someone's defensive attitude, which results from fear of failure. The third reason has to do with exhaustion (especially in managers); too busy, too much stress, too much tension, too little time for themselves, insufficient balance between work and life, and family problems. Various solutions could be put forward for these problems, such as better communication with others at work, a healthier situation at home, better use of free time and regularly performing the breathing and silence exercise. Formulating the PBSC in combination with performing this exercise, implementation of your PBSC in accordance with the PDAC cycle, and introduction of an ambition meeting will prevent these problems. On the basis of the PBSC approach you will also be able to manage your spare time in a more structured fashion so that you can enjoy optimum experiences and new challenges at home. This will also help with your hobbies, which require specific skills, behaviors and inner discipline. Robert Park, the prominent American sociologist said 60 years ago, *"I suspect that the biggest waste of American life flows from squandering of our spare time."*

Relevant to this are some important statements made by Mihaly Csikszentmihalyi:

> Together we squander the equivalent of millions of years of human consciousness. The energy which can be used for concentration on complex objectives, personal growth and feeling well, is being dissipated on incentives which do not do more than imitate reality.... Work and spare time can also provide for our needs. People, who learn to enjoy their work, and use their spare time the right way, often have the idea that their lives have become more valuable. The future is not only for the learned person, but also for the person who has learned to use his spare time effectively.

Mihaly Csikszentmihalyi's research has also shown that the average American works only 30 hours a week and uses 19 hours in spare time activities. This spare time consists of activities divided in the following manner—watching TV/being on line—seven hours, reading—three hours, jogging/bowling/playing music—two hours and social activities, such as parties, movies, being with family, gossiping with acquaintances or talking with friends—seven hours. The remaining 50–60 waking hours in the week are used for support activities, such as eating, commuting, shopping, doing laundry, repairing, and staring out of the window. Research suggests that the ability to browse web pages at high speed, download files such as music or films and play online games is changing what people do in their spare time. A large scale study by Jupiter Research suggested that broadband was changing television viewing habits. In homes with broadband, 40% said they were spending less time watching TV. The threat to TV was greatest in countries where broadband was on the rise, in particular the UK, France and Spain. TV companies are facing a major threat over the next 5 years, with broadband being predicted to increase its access from 19% to 37% of households by 2009.

Valuable energy is wasted in spending time on activities that are of no value and on daydreaming. There are many important and fun things to do in life. The challenge is to respect time, so that we can achieve a fuller, more satisfying life. According to Robin Sharma—

> True happiness comes from only one thing: achievement of goals, whether they are personal, professional or otherwise. You are happiest when you feel you are growing. When you feel that you are contributing and advancing in the direction of your dreams, you will notice that you have boundless energy and vitality. Time spent on activities which offer little reward aside from a fleeting feeling of relaxation (television watching is the best example), is time lost forever. Relaxation is essential but choose the most effective means of renewal and spend your time in productive pursuits that will slowly move you along the path of accomplishment. Happiness comes from doing—not sleeping.

Also remember what Charles Darwin said—*"Anyone who dares to waste one hour of life has not discovered the value of life."*

Many of the above-mentioned spare time activities are often not challenging and do not result in an optimum flow experience, because challenges and skills needed for these are not always on a high level. Chances to be happier, more joyful, more creative, more satisfied, and to stimulate personal growth in spare time are often missed in pursuit of these activities. Therefore it is recommended that you systematically apply both the PBSC method and the PDAC cycle not only at your workplace but also in your spare time and with your family. You will then be able to realize your family objectives and to breathe more life into your relationships with your spouse and children. Hence, assist your family members in formulating their PBSC, let them share it amongst themselves, and stimulate them to perform the breathing and silence exercise. You will thus create conditions so that you can enjoy life with your family and be happy together. Work-life balance is also an important issue that employers must offer in order to retain and develop talent. Many companies in North America and Europe have been successful in allowing employees to schedule their own shifts, so as to be able to meet family commitments. Research shows that one of the reasons why partners broke up was that they spent too much time on their careers (*http://www.asanet.org/media/timewarp.html*). People want more time for themselves and their kids now. According to U.S. Census figures, the average male is stated to have worked 43.5 hours a week in 1970 and 43.1 hours a week in 2000, and the average female 37.1 hours in 1970 and 37.0 hours in 2000.

The average U.S. worker wastes more than two hours a day, and that's not including lunch, according to a new Web survey by America On-line and Salary.com. That means companies spend as much as $759 billion (U.S.) on salaries annually for which they receive no apparent benefit, the research found.

Discipline yourself and stop wasting time on unimportant tasks and concentrate on those activities that are truly meaningful for your life's ambition. Such activities include self-learning, selfrenewal and reflection, forging relationships built on trust and mutual respect, physical fitness, reading and thinking deeply, and serving others. The PBSC will help you organize your time effectively. It allows you to accomplish those goals, which are truly important as well as enjoy leisure time. Good time management offers more time for challenging fun and relaxation. Another thing aimed at with the introduction of the PBSC method is to increase the inner involvement of workers at their workplace, so that they will be able to use their mental capacity better and show higher productivity. Physical presence on the job but without inner involvement and engagement (and therefore without optimal performance)—*mental absence* is the cause of one of the largest uncontrolled expenses in organizations today. The annual financial loss in the US due to disengagement of managers and employees is about $300B US (The Gallup Poll, 2005).

In seven countries (UK, USA, Sweden, Netherlands, India, Hong Kong and Australia) SHL, the world leader in providing psychometric assessment techniques, asked hundreds of managers how much time they spent managing 'poor performers'. This time, in the Netherlands alone, corresponds to the equivalent of approximately US$ 13 billion every year in management salaries, without even counting the direct damage caused by underperformance. In its 2004 research study, it was found that the cost of bad performance by employees costs as much as US$ 32 billion in the UK. This is related to the lack of motivation and inner involvement since there is no concordance between personal ambition and shared ambition. Unfortunately this is not a British problem alone. Compared to 1.6% of GDP losses in the UK, the losses in Hong Kong are a staggering 2.99%, with the US losing 1.05% and Sweden a still substantial 0.59%.

It was proven through Mihaly Csikszentmihalyi's research that the average American devotes 10% of working hours on irrelevant matters, such as daydreaming and gossiping with colleagues. In some cases, this even goes as high as 25% of work time. Experience teaches us that the PBSC concept and the match between personal ambition and shared ambition is a good solution for the problems discussed. I am introducing two strategies to bring about this match—

1. Introduction of a voluntary, informal and confidential ambition meeting between the line-manager and his/her employee, with the PBSC of the employee and the shared ambition as topics. This meeting takes place periodically, with a minimum frequency of once per quarter, or once in every two or three months.
2. Integration of the PBSC with the job-oriented talent development process (see Chapter 8). This approach will change the organizational culture (i.e. the shared values and beliefs which result in a certain way of doing things and a distinct environment), which will continually impact the employee's transformational process. It will work as a catalyst to accelerate the transformation of satisfied workers into committed employees. Before going deeper into this process I want to first explain the concept of shared ambition.

SHARED AMBITION

My most important wish is that the global business community could adopt a shared vision for the next 10 to 20 years about what you want the world to look like, and then go about trying to create it in ways that actually enhance your business, but do so in other people as well. I think the factor about globalization that tends to be underappreciated is, it will only work if we understand it genuinely means interdependence. It means interdependence, which means that none of us who are fortunate can any longer help ourselves unless we are prepared to help our neighbors. And we need a more unifying, more inclusive vision. Once you know where you're going, it's a lot easier to decide what steps to take to get there. If you don't know where you're going, you can work like crazy and you would be walking in the wrong direction.

—Bill Clinton, former President of the USA

Shared ambition is comprised of the first three parts of the Organizational Balanced Scorecard (OBSC), namely, organizational mission, vision and core values. The OBSC is a top-down management instrument that is used for making an organization's strategic vision operational at all organizational levels. It includes the overall (corporate) organizational mission, vision, core values, critical success factors, objectives, performance measures, targets and improvement actions, which are divided according to the four basic perspectives (Rampersad, 2003). The OBSC is a participatory approach that provides a framework for the systematic development of business strategy. It makes the shared ambition measurable and translates it systematically into actions. The OBSC system as part of the Total Performance Scorecard (TPS) concept differs from the basis BSC concept of Robert Kaplan and David Norton (developed in the early 1990s) on the following point—the critical success factors in the OBSC form a bridge between the organizational mission, vision and core values and the remaining elements in this concept, while in the latter, this link is not made explicit. The OBSC concept also includes a clear link to human capital. In the BSC concept, this link is not explicit—this may also be factor responsible for underperformance in BSC implementation.

There are indications that many implementations of the BSC in North America have been disappointing at best, and in Europe and South America even more so (Angel & Rampersad, 2005). An estimated 65%–70% of organizations within Corporate Canada have adopted the BSC or something like it. A few users—around 10%—state their scorecards are achieving positive results and respond to suggestions that balanced scorecards do not work with spirited rebuttal. However, a much larger group doubts that scorecards achieve sustained improvement in financial performance. Our view (based on hands-on experience) is that scorecards rarely achieve sustained financial improvement. BSC implementations tend to be insufficiently committed to learning and rarely take the personal ambitions of employees into account. We do not argue that Kaplan & Norton's BSC is fundamentally inappropriate as a management tool. On the contrary, we support the idea—but with a modified approach, using the TPS and OBSC concepts, in order to achieve an implementation that has produced better results empirically. Our position is that organizational scorecards need to be aligned with individuals' scorecards so that the BSC is turned into a powerful tool for sustained organizational performance.

Our conclusion based on 20 years of research is that scorecard performance depends on alignment between the goals of the organization and the personal goals of the employees to realize performance change. What we are referring to is the aligning of individuals' personal ambition with the shared ambition, which is a prerequisite for sustainable cultural change and for the development of organizations. Alignment means linking the organization's mission, vision, and core values with the individual's personal mission, vision, and key roles. This lies at the heart of successful organizational change and development. Traditional BSC implementations tend to be insufficiently committed to learning, and rarely take the personal ambitions of the employee into account. Without a set of rules for employees to address continuous improvement in the process as well as the personal improvement of individual employees, the experience has been that too few employees buy in, and there is insufficient change in the organization's culture; this underlies the BSC's disappointing performance. The result as seen in so many BSC implementations is that any improvements tend to be superficial and temporary. We have seen many examples of BSCs (banks, airlines, insurance companies, government agencies, etc.) which did not achieve alignment and resulted in an apparent performance improvement that dissipated very quickly.

In other cases, the improvement never even materialized. Frequently, management's efforts to improve performance were seen as divisive, viewed by employees as aimed at benefiting senior management compensation plans and fostering a "what's in it for me" attitude among the employees. In the aligned environment, metrics needs to support the people alignment to organizational alignment. The boxed text below shows ten reasons for BSC failures based on Kaplan and Norton's traditional BSC (Angel & Rampersad, 2005).

Ten Reasons for Balanced Scorecard Failures

1. Accounting approach with a systematic neglect of the human capital; no linkage between the critical success factors of the organization and the personal critical success factors of individual employees— creating human capital tensions between work and non-work aspirations.
2. Emphasis mainly on financial measures rather than non-financial, leading to measures that do not connect to the drivers of the business and are not relevant to performance improvement.
3. No explicit link between shared ambition and specific organizational objectives; results in insufficient employee support to work according to organizational performance measures and an implementation plan that is not grounded in reality and unable to respond quickly to unforeseen events.
4. No explicit link between personal ambition and ethical behavior; a systematic neglect of personal integrity.
5. No explicit link between personal ambition and shared ambition.
6. Poor communication of the new way of working by management; results in creation of an employee mentality that is hostile to management messages.
7. Results in an individual performance plan that focuses too much on the money side and not enough on delivering organizational values, leading to a "what's in it for me" culture.
8. Self learning and team learning are not stimulated; results in creation of a climate of defensiveness and mistrust and a business strategy that is poorly understood and therefore impossible to execute.
9. Too many objectives defined and too many performance metrics being measured.
10. Data on current individual and organizational performance insufficiently available; poor data on actual performance, negating most of the effort invested in defining performance measures by not being able to monitor actual changes in results from changes in behavior.

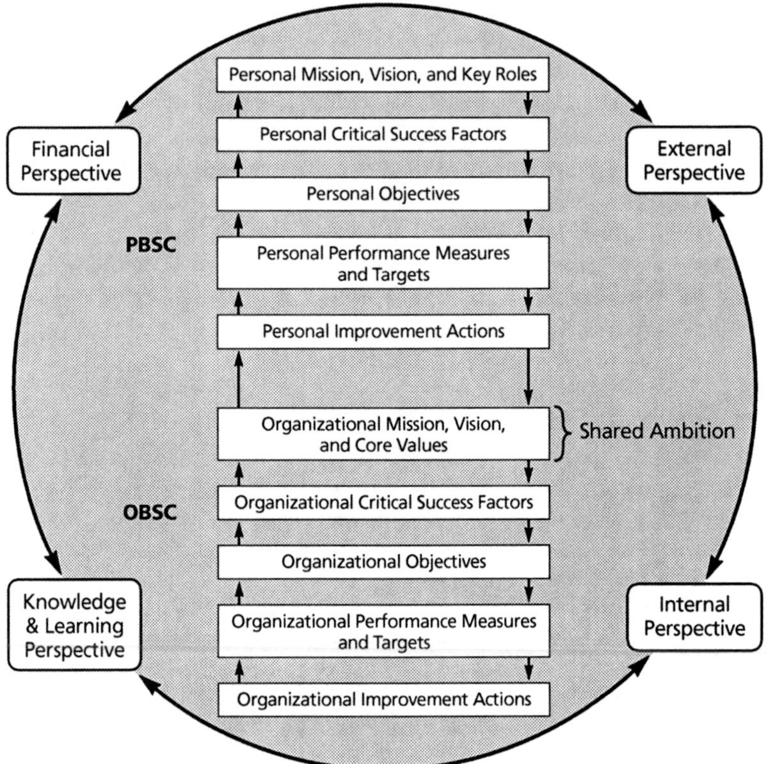

Figure 5.2. Model of the Personal and Organizational Balanced Scorecard (Rampersad, 2003)

It has been shown that organizational development in accordance with the OBSC and Total Performance Scorecard concept can address these issues. I now want to further explain my OBSC concept. The four result domains in the OBSC include categories of business results, which are of essential importance for survival. As with the PBSC, the following 4 basic perspectives have been chosen; however, the contents have different meanings—

1. *Financial*: Financial soundness. How do shareholders see the company? What does it mean for our shareholders?
2. *External*: Customer satisfaction. How do customers see the company? What does it mean for our customers?
3. *Internal*: Process control. How can we control the primary business processes in order to create value for our customers? In which processes do we have to excel to continuously satisfy our customers?

4. *Knowledge and learning*: Skills and attitudes of the employees and the organizational learning ability. How can the company remain successful in the future? How should we learn and improve, and through this continuously realize our shared ambition?

These four basic perspectives also cover the consequences for the community. It would be too much to go into detail about the OBSC concept in the framework of this book. For more information about the OBSC, I refer you to my book *Total Performance Scorecard* (2003). A brief overview is given in the box that follows. The elements of the OBSC and PBSC and their mutual connection, are shown in Figure 5.2. Figure 5.3 shows the elements of the OBSC.

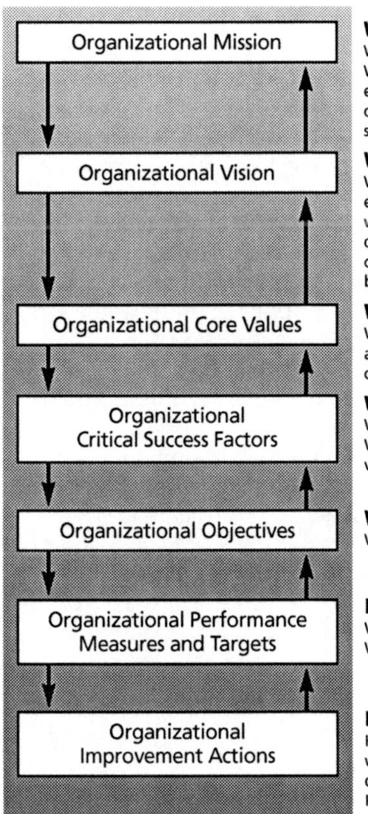

WHY DO WE EXIST?
Why does our organization exist? Who are we? What do we do? Where are we? What is our identity? What is the purpose of our existence? What is our primary function? What is our ultimate main objective? For whom do we exist? Who are our most important stakeholders? What fundamental need do we fulfill?

WHERE ARE WE GOING TOGETHER?
What is the most ambitious dream of our organization? How do we envision the future? What are our long-term ambitions? What do we want to achieve? Where do we go from here? How do we see a desirable and achievable shared future situation, and what are the change routes needed to reach it? What changes lie ahead in the business landscape? Who do we want to be?

WHICH VALUES ARE PRECIOUS TO US?
What do we stand for? What connects us? What is important in our attitude? What do we believe in? How do we treat each other? How do we work together? How do we think of ourselves?

WHICH FACTORS MAKE US UNIQUE?
What is the most important factor of our organizational success? Which organizational factors are essential for our organizational viability? What are our core competencies?

WHAT RESULTS DO WE WANT?
Which short-term measurable results must we achieve?

HOW CAN WE MEASURE THE RESULTS?
What makes the organizational vision and objectives measurable? Which values must be obtained? What are the targets?

HOW DO WE WANT TO ACHIEVE THE RESULTS?
How can we realize the objectives? Which improvement actions are we going to implement? How do we create a platform for the developed strategies? How will we communicate this to the people? How do we see that we learn continuously?

Figure 5.3. Elements of the Organizational Balanced Scorecard (Rampersad, 2003)

The Organizational Balanced Scorecard

Organizational Mission

The organizational mission consists of an organization's identity and indicates its reason for existing: Why, to what extent, and for whom does it exist? What are the primary function and the ultimate objective of the organization? Which basic need does it fulfill, and who are its most important stakeholders? An effectively formulated mission creates a sense of unity in the behavior of employees, strengthens their like-mindedness, and improves both communication and the atmosphere within the organization.

Organizational Vision

The organizational vision contains the most ambitious dream of the organization. It provides a shared vision of a desired and feasible future, as well as the route needed to reach it. It indicates what the organization wants to achieve, what is essential for its success, and which critical success factors make it unique. Standards, values, and principles are also part of the organizational vision. The vision, in contrast to the mission, is tied to a timeline. An effectively formulated vision guides personal ambitions and creativity, establishes a climate that is fertile for change, strengthens the organization's belief in the future, and therefore releases energy in people. Together the organizational mission and vision express the soul of the organization. Together with the Core Values (see below), they form its shared organizational ambition and have an important impact on the relationship between the employees and the organization. A successfully formulated organizational ambition shows people how their activities contribute to the larger whole. People working together towards strategic objectives often produce better performances. They feel pride in making a useful contribution towards something worthwhile. The organizational mission and vision direct an organization and function both as its compass and its road map. They also make employees proud of their organization, letting them focus on relevant activities and in turn create value for customers, thus eliminating unproductive activities. In an organization without a mission and vision, employees are exposed to ad hoc decisions and short-term plans.

Organizational Core Values

The organizational vision is also based on a set of shared values that are used to strengthen the like-mindedness, commitment, and devotion of employees and to influence their behavior positively. These core values determine how one must act in order to realize the organizational vision. They function as the guiding principles that support people's behavior at work. Core values hold people together if they act and think along the lines of these values. They articulate the way we treat each other and how we see customers, employees, shareholders, suppliers, and the community. If the principles, norms, and values of the employees match those of the organization, then their efforts and involvement would be optimal. Therefore, core values are strongly related to the personal ambition of the individual employees. After all, with an organizational mission and vision based on shared values, the personal objectives of individual employees will correspond closely to those of the organization. The core value must be ethical in order to pass the test of moral scrutiny. Everyone within the organization should act in accordance with these principles and moral standards. Jack Welch formulated five core values to change General Electric—loathing bureaucracy and all nonsense associated with it; understanding what is meant by responsibility and devotion and decisiveness; determining aggressive objectives and realizing them with energetic integrity; having the faith to empower others; and nothing is a secret. Konosuke Matsushita, the maker of modern Japan, formulated seven spiritual values for the Matsushita Electric Co. (also to develop new business ethics for Japan)—national service through industry, fairness, harmony and cooperation, struggle for betterment, courtesy and humility, adjustment and assimilation, and gratitude.

Organizational Critical Success Factors

An organizational critical success factor is one in which the organization must excel in order to survive, or one that is of overriding importance to organizational success. Such strategic issues determine the competitive advantage of an organization. They are factors in which the organization wants to differ and make itself unique in the market, and as such are related to its core competencies. Critical success factors are also related to the four previously mentioned OBSC perspectives and thus form an integral part of the shared ambition. In this ambition you will always find a set of critical success factors, which is related to the four perspectives. The critical success factors form the link between the organizational mission, vision, and core values and the remaining OBSC elements. This link is made by identifying the core competencies in the shared ambition and by including these four perspectives in the OBSC table. The core competencies are then translated into organizational objectives. The shared ambition, therefore, has a minimum of four critical success factors (minimum one per perspective), every critical success factor has one or more related objectives, each objective has a maximum of two related performance measures, every performance measure has only one related target, which in turn is linked to one or more related improvement actions. Examples of organizational critical success factors are: financially strong and healthy; well-motivated personnel; a stimulating working environment; skilled employees; teamwork; customer orientation; good customer service; top position in certain markets; image; high product quality.

Organizational Objectives

Organizational objectives are measurable results that must be achieved. They describe the expected results that should be achieved within a short time in order to realize the long-term shared ambition. These objectives are derived directly from the critical success factors and form realistic milestones. The objectives are formulated through a SWOT analysis. Quantifying objectives is avoided in the OBSC; it will take place at a later phase via performance measures and targets. The objectives form part of a cause-and-effect chain, resulting in the final organizational objective. In this respect, I would like to refer to the words of Konoshuke Matsushita—*"Profit should not be reflected of corporate greed but a vote of confidence from society that what is offered by the firm is valued."*

In my view employees come first, the customers come second, and the shareholders are in third place. You will not improve the quality of life of your customers and shareholders and make them happy, if you do not first improve the quality of life of your employees and make them happy. The organization should be stakeholder-oriented instead of shareholder-oriented. A study performed by Harvard Business School found that companies that were stakeholder-oriented meaning that they paid explicit attention to their responsibilities to their stakeholders, such as employees, customers, society, the environment, and their shareholders showed four times the growth rate and eight times the employment growth than those companies that only focused on increasing the wealth of their shareholders (Miller and Pruzan, 2003). Wealth creation is not a major objective; it's the means by which we can serve the society.

Organizational Performance Measures

An organizational performance measure is an indicator, related to a critical success factor and a strategic objective, and is used to judge the functioning of a specific process. These indicators are the standards by which the progress of the strategic objectives is measured. They are essential when putting strategic plans into action. When they are interconnected so that managers can deduce a certain course of action from them, they provide management with timely signals of organizational guidance, based on the measurement of (process) changes and the comparison of the measured results to the norms. Therefore, performance measures make the organizational vision and objectives measurable.

Organizational Targets

An organizational target is the quantitative objective of a performance measure. It is a value that an organization aspires towards, the realization of which can be measured by means of a performance measure. In other words, targets indicate values to be obtained.

> ***Organizational Improvement Actions***
>
> Organizational improvement actions are strategies undertaken to realize the organizational ambition. The how is central here. Alternative strategies are formed on the basis of the aforementioned OBSC-steps, and from this, actions are chosen which result in the greatest contribution to the critical success factors.
>
> The OBSC I have defined as the following formula—
>
> OBSC = organizational mission + vision + core values + critical success factors + objectives + performance measures + targets + improvement actions (divided along the four perspectives: financial, external, internal, and knowledge & learning).
>
> *Source: Total Performance Scorecard; Redefining Management to Achieve Performance with Integrity* (Rampersad, 2003).

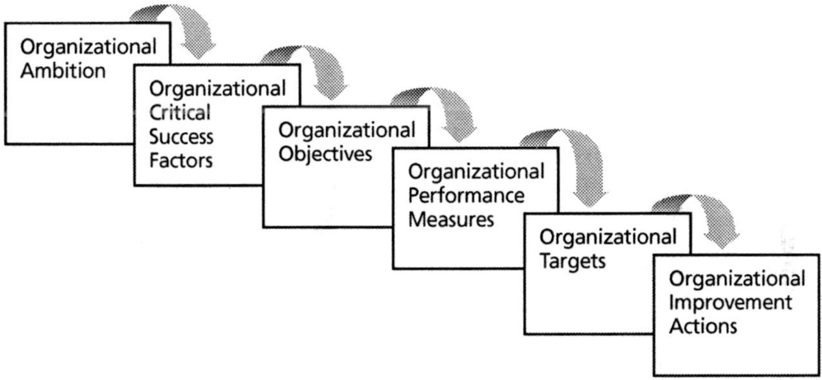

Figure 5.4. Relationships between OBSC-elements

You will find the shared ambition of Business Jet; an airliner for business people in the next box to illustrate the foregoing. The translation of this shared ambition into action (the OBSC) can be found in my book *Total Performance Scorecard; Redefining Management to Achieve Performance with Integrity* (Rampersad, 2003).

Shared Ambition of Business Jet

Organizational Mission

We are a safe and reliable airline company for business people.

Organizational Vision

In all aspects we want to be a professional organization, one that is the customers. first choice for business travel in all the regions where we operate. We want to achieve this by:

1. Achieving excellent financial results through the successful introduction of innovative products and services;
2. Offering our customers high-quality services and, thanks to our image, having a dominant share in the global market of business travel;
3. Having airplanes depart and arrive on time, doing so more successfully than competitors;
4. Creating an inspiring work environment that provides an atmosphere of team spirit, open communication, and process thinking;
5. Continuously developing our human potential, and, based on our knowledge, skills, and capabilities, acquiring competitive advantage.

In order to be the safest and most reliable business travel company, everything within our organization will be focused on achieving top performance with a motivated work force that cares for the needs of the society we are part of.

Core Values

We are being led by the following core values:

- *Integrity:* Doing business with integrity. Integrity is never compromised
- *Enjoyment and Passion*: Working with devoted people who enjoy their work, are passionate, and are driven to achieve superior performances in everything our company undertakes. Employee engagement is our way of life
- *Customer Orientation:* Listening continuously to our customers, discovering their expectations and providing them with the quality services they expect of us, and satisfying them constantly. They are the focus of everything we do
- *Safe and Reliable:* Being known as the safest and most reliable airline company

AMBITION MEETING

The glue that holds all relationships together—including the relationship between the leader and the led is trust, and trust is based on integrity.

—Brian Tracy

Experience tells us that workers are often willing to work together towards the goals of the organization with dedication when there is a match between their personal ambition and the shared ambition of their organization. It is, therefore, recommended to encourage managers and employees to formulate their personal ambition and to let them reflect about the balance between their own personal ambition and the shared ambition. I, therefore, recommend introducing an *ambition meeting* within organizations between the line-manager or superior and his/her employees. The ambition meeting is a periodical, informal, voluntary and confidential meeting of a maximum duration of one hour between line-manager and his/her employees, with the employee's PBSC and the shared ambition as topics. *Why informal? Because you learn the most from informal than from formal meetings.* It is recommended that the meeting is held structurally at least once in three months, preferably more often. The outcome of these informal meetings should be highly confidential and should be kept out of the personnel file and not be used against the employee. The manager functions as a trusted person or informal coach. *Why as a trusted person? Because where there is distrust and fear, there is no learning.* To be able to talk about the employee's PBSC, one needs a confidential, informal and friendly atmosphere, an atmosphere of trust and open communication. This is essential as human values will be discussed. Experience has shown that this intimate atmosphere can be reached if the manager formulates his/her own PBSC beforehand and shares it with his/her employee. The implementation of the employee's PBSC comes up for discussion, and includes private matters, as well as work-related aspects. At least those private matters that have an impact on job performance will be discussed confidentially. The line-manager can make a selection of the following ambition questions, which he/she can use during in the ambition meeting—

- Does your personal ambition correspond with the shared ambition?
- Can you identify yourself with the shared ambition? In doing this, do you feel personally involved and addressed by the shared ambition? Are your personal mission, vision, and key roles to be found in the shared ambition? If not, do they have to be expanded or adjusted? Are they acceptable? How can they flourish within the organization?
- Is it possible that your personal ambition level or that of the organization should be lowered?
- Do your personal values and principles match the organizational vision and core values? If they conflict, is leaving the best answer? Are your most important personal values done justice to here? Which points in your personal ambition are strengthening and which conflict with the shared ambition? Which ones are neglected?

- Is there a win-win situation between your own interests and the ones of your organization?
- Which skills do you need to be a pillar of the organization and thus realize the shared ambition? What do you want to gain through this?
- Are your developmental expectations in tune with those of the organization?
- Do your job requirements match your capabilities and needs?
- How is the implementation of your PBSC going? Did you reach your target? Could it be better? Where did it go wrong? What have you learned? What did you unlearn?
- What motivates you? What demotivates you? What makes you happy or sad? What do you enjoy the most? Where do you stand and where do you want to go? What prevents me from being who you want to be and what you want to be? What do you most want to learn? What do you very much like to do? What do you really want? What gives you satisfaction? In which kind of environment do you prefer to be? What do you want to be in this organization? Which contribution are you trying to make to the realization of our shared ambition? To which job do you aspire? What are your wishes? What do you strive for? What are your concerns?
- Do you have ethical problems on the job?
- Have you considered a job change because of this?

Many people decided to look for another job after participating in our TPS and PBSC seminars, after they have discovered themselves and have tried to align their personal ambition with the organization's shared ambition. Sometimes this can be the best option for both yourself and the organization. During the alignment process, the manager should provide social support to the employees by being a good listener, providing help, and being someone the employee can rely on. Free and open communication within the company is an important issue here. Steve Jobs stated during his time at Apple Computer—

> I believe strongly in open communication within the firm. All employees have complete access to almost all information in the company, including other employees' salaries. Only when employees understand the entire master plan for the firm they will be able to make effective decisions that are in line with the company's values.

Aligning personal ambition with shared ambition deals with the mutual concordance of the Personal and Organizational Balanced Scorecards or individual and collective learning (see Figure 5.5). This has an impact on the organizational bonding of the employees. It gives them the proud feeling that they count (that they are being paid attention), that they are

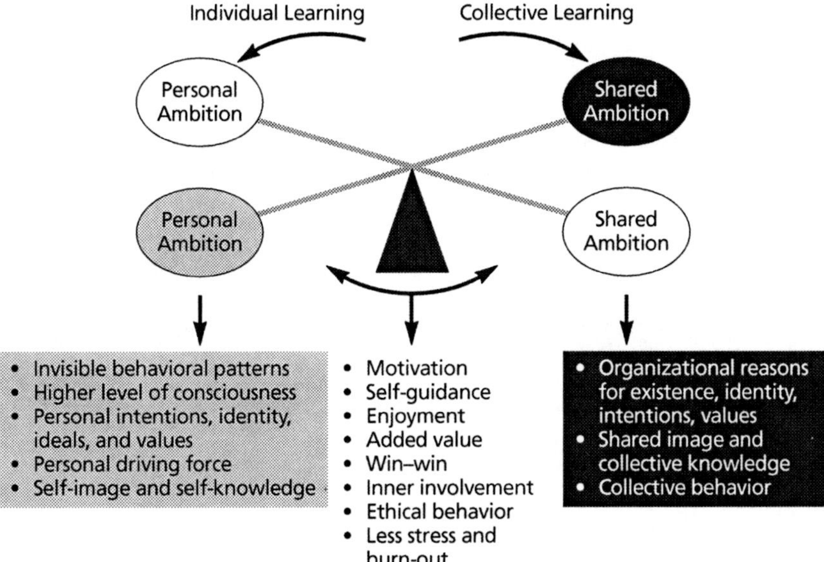

Figure 5.5. Aligning Personal Ambition with Shared Ambition

appreciated as human beings and that they make a useful and valuable contribution to the organization. Employees are stimulated in this way to commitment,

dedication and to focus on those activities which create value for clients. This will create a foundation of peace and stability upon which creativity and growth can flourish. The alignment of the personal ambition with the shared organizational ambition has to do with reaching a high degree of compatibility between the PBSC and the OBSC, as shown in Figure 5.6.

Formula for Right Personal Action within the Organization

The concordance between personal ambition and personal behavior on the one hand and personal and shared ambition on the other, ensures that your organizational actions are *right*. I have defined this as (Rampersad, 2005)—

Right personal action within your organization =
Being + PBSC + Doing + Aligning personal ambition with personal behavior + Aligning personal ambition with shared ambition

This formula entails action (doing), which stems from your being, insight into yourself on the basis of your PBSC, taking on challenges, the balance between your personal ambition and your ethical behavior (see previous chapter) and the balance between personal ambition and the shared ambition in order to enjoy your work.

In the next chapter, I will discuss the third alignment in the PBSC system, that between shared ambition and business ethics. Business ethics is related to personal integrity, which I discussed in Chapter 4.

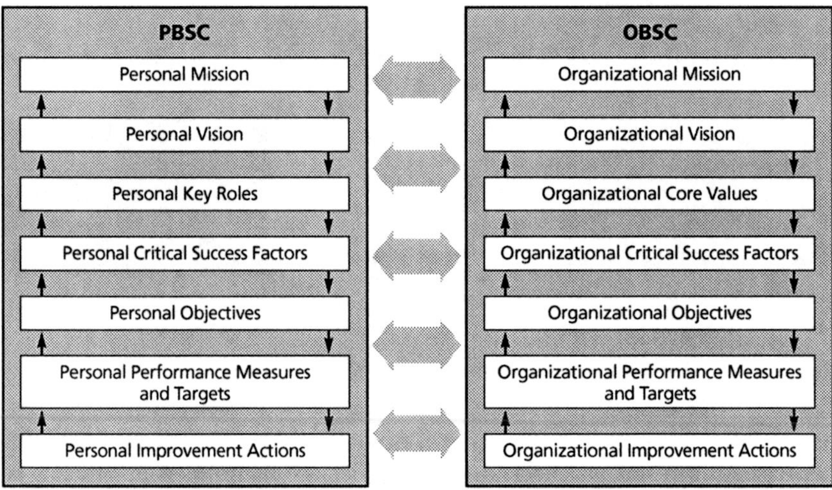

Figure 5.6. Aligning PBSC with OBSC

CHAPTER 6

ALIGNING PERSONAL AND SHARED AMBITION WITH BUSINESS ETHICS, SHARED INTEGRITY

At this moment, America's highest economic need is higher ethical standards—standards enforces by strict laws and upheld by responsible business leaders"

—George W. Bush, President of the United States, Corporate Responsibility Speech, July 9, 2002

Our market system depends critically on trust—trust in the world of our colleagues and trust in the world of those with whom we do business.... I am saying that the state of corporate governance to a very large extent reflects the character of the CEO.

—Alan Greenspan, Former Chairman of the Board of Governors of the Federal Reserve System

Business or corporate ethics is a term that defines how a company integrates its shared ambition and the personal integrity of individuals into its policies, practices, and decision-making. In Chapter 4, I introduced a practical framework for the development of personal integrity. The next step is to integrate the personal integrity of individuals into a system called shared integrity. The scope of business ethics has expanded to encompass a company's actions with regard to the nature and quality of the relationships it wishes to have with all its stakeholders. Stakeholders should care about eth-

Personal Balanced Scorecard, pages 111–121

ics and corporate social responsibility, and ensure that their actions reflect integrity and high ethical standards. Ethics guide human duty and the principles on which it is based (Thompson & Strickland, 2002). Regarding regulation and legislation such as the Sarbanes-Oxley Act, it is now recognized that every company has an ethical (and legal) duty to its shareholders, employees, customers, suppliers, the community, the environment, indigenous peoples, and even future generations. Each of these stakeholders affects the organization and is, in turn, affected by it.

The duty to shareholders arises out of the expectation of a superior return on investment and improved dividend payment. It is the moral duty of business executives and employees to create a profitable organization based on owner investment. A company's ethical duty to its employees arises out of respect for the worth and dignity of individuals who devote their energy to the business. Business executives also have the moral duty to promote employee interests such as competence development, career opportunities, job security and good working conditions. The ethical duty to the customer encompasses the provision of adequate products or services according to liability laws, and based on high standards. Organizations also have the moral duty to protect customers by, for example, voluntarily informing them about the ingredients in their products, whether or not they have potential harmful effects, and by recalling products they suspect to have faulty parts or defective designs. The duty to suppliers arises out of their partnership that is needed to realize high product quality. Companies confront several ethical issues in their supplier relationships. For example, is it ethical to purchase goods from suppliers who employ child laborers, pay low wages or have poor working conditions? The ethical duty of the company to the community at large arises out of the fact that, as a member of the society, the organization is expected to be a good citizen. This is demonstrated by, for instance, paying taxes, having eco-consciousness, supporting community activities and creating job opportunities. To quote N. R. Narayana Murthy, Chairman of Infosys Technologies Limited: *"We are all aware of our rights as citizens. Nevertheless, we often fail to acknowledge the duty that accompanies every right. Our duty is towards the community as a whole, as much as it is towards our families."*

The most important business ethics issues faced by companies are—corruption and bribery, financial and accounting integrity, consumer and employee privacy, ethical advertising, and conflicts of interest. A series of accounting scandals in the past years rocked the corporate world, damaged stock markets, destroyed major companies and led to fines and prison terms for executives. Enron is an example of a successful company that went into bankruptcy because it was undermined by its management's unethical behavior (see boxed text below). It emphasizes the importance of balancing the personal ambition of management and employees with their personal behavior and with the shared ambition.

Enron

A Bold Shared Ambition Undermined by Its Management's Unethical Behavior

Until its crash in the fall of 2001, Enron was one of the world's largest electricity, natural gas and broadband trading companies, with revenues of more than $100 billion. Enron's strategic intent was to become the blue-chip energy and communications company of the twenty-first century through its business efforts in four core areas—Enron wholesale, Enron broadband, Enron energy and Enron transportation. Enron management claimed that each of these business units supported the company's shared ambition. This was stated as follows—

Who are we and why do we exist? We offer a wide range of physical, transportation, financial and technical solutions to thousands of customers around the world. Our business is to create value and opportunity for your business. We do this by combining our financial resources, access to physical commodities, and knowledge to create innovative solutions to challenging industrial problems. We are best known for our natural gas and electricity products, but today we also offer retail energy and bandwidth products. These products give customers the flexibility they need to compete.

What we believe? We begin with a fundamental belief in the inherent wisdom of open markets. We are convinced that consumer choice and competition lead to lower prices and innovation. Enron is a laboratory for innovation. That is why we employ the best and the brightest people. And we believe that every employee can make a difference here. We encourage people to make a difference by creating an environment where everyone is allowed to achieve their full potential and where everyone has a stake in the outcome. We think this entrepreneurial approach stimulates creativity. We value diversity. We are committed to removing all barriers to employment and advancement based on sex, sexual orientation, race, religion, age, ethnic background, national origin or physical limitation. Our success is measured by the success of our customers. We are committed to meeting their energy needs with solutions that offer them a competitive advantage. And we work with them in ways that reinforce the benefits of a long-term partnership with Enron. In everything we do, we operate safely and with concern for the environment. This is a responsibility we take seriously in all the different places around the world where we do business. We are changing the way energy is delivered, as well as the market for it. We are reinventing the fundamentals of this business by providing energy at lower costs and in more usable forms than it has been provided before. Everything we do is about change. Together we are creating the leading energy company in the world. Together, we are defining the energy company of the future.

Our core values of integrity, respect, excellence and communication. We work with customers and prospects openly, honestly and sincerely. When we say we will do something, we do it; when we say we cannot or will not do something, we will not do it. We treat others as we would like to be treated ourselves. We do not tolerate abusive or disrespectful treatment. Ruthlessness, callousness, and arrogance do not belong here. We are satisfied with nothing less than the very best in everything we do. We will continue to raise the bar for everyone. The great fun here will be for all of us to discover just how good we can really be. We have an obligation to communicate. Here, we take time to talk with one another and to listen. We believe that information is meant to move and that information moves people.

Gaping flaws in Enron's strategy began to emerge in fall 2001, starting with revelations that the company had incurred billions in debt to increase its energy trading business, far more than was first apparent from its balance sheet. The off-balance-sheet debt was hidden by obscurely worded footnotes to the company's financial statements, involving mysterious partnerships in which the company's chief financial officer (CFO) had a personal interest. After Enron's stock price slid from the mid-$80s to the high-$30s, despite glowing earnings reports, the company's well-regarded chief executive officer resigned for .personal reasons. in August 2001. Weeks later, the company's CFO was asked to resign when details of his conflict of interest in the off-balance-sheet partnerships came to light. Meanwhile, top company executives continued to insist publicly that the company was in sound financial shape and that its business was secure, hoping to keep customers from shifting their business to rivals and to reassure concerned shareholders.

But Enron's crown jewel, its energy trading business (which generated about $60 billion in reported revenues), came under increased scrutiny, both for the debt that had been amassed to support such enormous trading volumes and for its thin profit margins, some of which were suspect because of accounting methods approved of by Arthur Andersen, the company's auditor. Within weeks, Enron filed for bankruptcy. Its stock price fell below $1 per share, its stock was de-listed from the New York Stock Exchange and a scandal of enormous proportions resulted.

Arthur Anderson fired the partner on the Enron account when it appeared that working papers related to the audit were destroyed in an apparent effort to obstruct a congressional investigation of Enron's collapse. Enron's board fired Arthur Anderson as the company's auditor. Then Enron was caught destroying documents (as late as January 2002) in an apparent attempt to hide the company's actions from investigators. Enron's chairman and CEO resigned. The company's former vice-chairman committed suicide after it became public that he had vigorously protested Enron's accounting practices earlier in 2001. It also came out that senior company officers had sold shares of Enron months earlier, when the stocks. price first began to slide. Enron employees—most of whom had their entire 401,000 savings tied up in Enron stock and were precluded from selling their shares, and 4,000 of whom were dismissed in a last-ditch effort to cut costs—watched helplessly as their retirement savings were wiped out. The extent of management's unethical behavior is still under investigation. But Enron management clearly did not act in accordance with the principles and values it espoused.

(Thompson & Strickland, 2002, www.enron.com, 2000 company annual report)

According to Business for Social Responsibility (BSR, 2005) corporations should take a serious look at strengthening their ethics programs in order to (see also Rampersad, 2003)—

- *Avoid bankruptcy, fines, lawsuits and criminal charges*—the flood of corporate scandals in 2002 and 2003 is a stark reminder of the catastrophic risks involved with business ethics failures. Companies like Enron, Arthur Anderson, CitiGroup, and WorldCom face extensive class-action and individual lawsuits on behalf of investors and employees that may drag on for years. Their senior management and directors are also finding themselves the target of lawsuits and civil and criminal prosecution.
- *Protect and strengthen sales, brand image, and reputation*—a 2002 survey of consumers in 25 countries by Environics International found that more than one-third of consumers in countries surveyed believed that large companies "should do more than give money to solve social problems." The same study found that almost 50% of consumers had considered punishing a company based on its social actions, and that nearly 30% had actually avoided a company for that reason.
- *Strengthen employee loyalty and commitment*—a U.S. employee survey carried out in 2001 by Walker Information found that only 6% of employees who thought their senior management was unethical were inclined to stay with their companies, while 40% who believed their leaders were ethical wanted to stay. A multi-sector survey carried out in the United States by the Hudson Institute in 2000 found a positive correlation between high ethical standards, work commitment, and loyalty, and concluded that "employees who believe they work in an ethical environment are six times more likely to be loyal than workers who believe their organization is unethical." Another study of U.S. workers carried out by the Aon Loyalty Institute in 2000 found that when employees do not feel they can trust management,

giving them additional benefits has no significant effect on their commitment. Another Aon survey in 2002 showed worker confidence in management had dropped to its lowest level since the survey began in 1997. Extensive anecdotal evidence suggests that employees have more positive feelings about themselves and their work—and demonstrate greater loyalty—when they work for a company they view as having good values and ethical practices.

- *Protect the company, especially during times of stress and transition*—the Ethics Resource Center's 2000 National Business Ethics Survey found that ethics programs may be of greatest benefit during organizational transitions such as mergers, acquisitions, restructurings and other high-stress situations, when employees may not have a normal degree of management guidance, and are thrust into new situations and responsibilities. The survey reported that in transitioning organizations with ethics programs, 30% of employees said they had observed misconduct at work within the last year, compared to similar organizations with only a code of ethics or no program at all, where nearly 50% of employees observed misconduct.
- *Avoid loss of business*—as large companies increasingly look beyond their own ethical practices to those of their suppliers as well, firms that have poor ethics practices may find contracts cancelled or future business lost. For example, in 2001 Royal Dutch/Shell cancelled 100 contracts with companies that failed to adhere to its ethical, health and safety, and environmental policies. Governments may also cancel contracts or otherwise punish companies perceived to be unethical. In 1999 the Japanese government revoked Credit Suisse's business license in Japan for "misleading and inappropriate" financial accounting practices, involving US$4 billion in transactions. In 2002, the Canadian engineering firm Acres International was found guilty of passing bribes to an official in Lesotho.
- *Avoid prescriptive government regulation*—a Washington Post/ABC Inc. poll taken in the midst of the 2002 corporate scandals found that 75% of respondents believe that recent revelations about wrongdoing at Enron, WorldCom and others signal "broader problems with the way companies report their finances." To fix the problems, 53% said the government should enforce existing laws more strictly, while 30% think new laws governing financial reporting are necessary.
- *Limit vulnerability to activist pressure and boycotts*—Companies perceived to behave unethically toward shareholders, employees, the community, or other stakeholders are more likely to find themselves the target of activist pressure, boycotts, or even 'denial of service' attacks on their Internet operations. Conversely, companies with a demonstrated commitment to ethical behavior can accrue a kind of 'integ-

rity capital' among stakeholders and the general public. This can help them weather an individual episode of misconduct or other crises without lasting damage to their credibility or reputation. One example is Johnson & Johnson, which despite several public problems in 2001 and 2002 continued to be ranked among the best reputed U.S. companies.

- *Enjoy greater access to capital*—The Social Investment Forum reported that more than $2 trillion in assets in 2001 were managed in portfolios that screen for ethical, environmental, and other socially responsible practices. This represents nearly 12% of the $19.9 trillion professional management funds in the United States. Companies with a demonstrated commitment to ethical, social, and environmental responsibilities have access to a rapidly growing pool of capital that might not otherwise be available.

A variety of methods can be employed to improve business ethics, such as (BSR 2005, Rampersad 2003)—

- *Build ethics into the personal and shared ambition statement*—The emphasis in the ambition statement should be on unselfishness. It includes ethical principles, values, and standards such as integrity, reliability, trust, helpfulness, credibility, frankness, etc. This helps senior managers and employees understand that values and ethical standards are integral to all company operations as well as leisure activities
- *Stimulate everyone within the organization (most of all top management) to formulate their PBSC and to align their personal ambition with their personal behavior*—also, stimulate them to do this at home. Make them aware that they must not act in conflict with their conscience, at work or in their spare time. Help them to become better human beings. To borrow Dwight Eisenhower's words: *A people that values its privileges above its principles soon loses both.*
- *Commit the organization to ethical behavior*—top management must be openly committed to ethical conduct and must provide constant leadership in tending to and renewing the values of the organization. Everyone within the organization must be made aware of their own personal ambition and of the core values of the firm's ambition. Involvement and commitment of personnel at all organizational levels is important in order to develop higher levels of trust and pride. Senior managers should participate in training sessions, make ethics a regular element in speeches and presentations, and align their own behavior with company ethical standards. Engage the employees in the ethics process by creating a board ethics committee or corporate responsibility committee, and by placing ethics on the board agenda as a regular item for discussion. Consider special training to enable

directors to carry out their ethical responsibilities confidently. Many U.S. companies have instituted board ethics training in recent years, a move motivated in part by the 1996 Caremark decision, which established the precedent that directors may be held liable for corporate ethical transgressions.

- *Integrate ethics into all aspects of company communications*—develop communication programs with emphasis on personal and corporate ethics to inform and motivate employees, customers, suppliers, shareholders, and the general public. Leverage existing company infrastructure to demonstrate to employees that ethics is an integral part of all operations and decision-making. Bell South has integrated ethics and compliance training materials into multiple delivery sources including new employee orientations, management courses, sales training, business meetings, business plans, and other aspects of day-to-day business.
- *Develop an ethics code or code of business conduct*—it tells employees and managers how to act in various situations, and makes it clear that they will be expected to recognize the ethical dimensions of corporate policies and actions. It also includes what is required of employees, where leeway is allowed in decision-making, where employees can go for advice or to report possible violations, and which ethical issues are non-negotiable. Comprehensive codes are aligned with company values and applicable laws and address the full range of ethical dilemmas employees are likely to face. They should be updated regularly as new challenges emerge. A study of three hundred large corporations showed that companies that made a public commitment to their ethics codes outperformed companies that didn't make such a commitment by two to three times, as measured by market value added (Social Investment Forum, 1999).
- *Identify and renew company's core values*—companies without a clear set of core values find themselves at a disadvantage when developing ethics programs. Research shows that ethics programs are most effective when perceived by employees to be value-driven rather than simply compliance-driven, and that value-based programs are most effective in reducing unethical behavior, strengthening employee commitment, and making employees more willing to deliver bad news to managers. Many companies conduct regular company-wide initiatives that involve employees at all levels to renew company values and update them where appropriate. A number of leadership companies also distinguish which of their corporate values are ethical values (integrity, fairness, honesty) as opposed to performance values (innovation, leadership, low-cost), and make it clear to

employees that if these sets of values come into conflict, ethical values must prevail.

- *Set up board ethics and corporate social responsibility committees*—let ethics officers or other senior managers with ethics responsibilities report directly to the board. Ethics officers should have regular access to executive decision-makers. The basic functions of an ethics officer are—identification and renewal of values; development of an ethics code; training and education; and providing counsel and guidance to staff at all levels.
- *Establish hot lines for comments and complaints regarding unethical acts*—to process reports of unethical behavior. Employees should feel it is their duty to report violations. A growing number of leadership companies take this one step further by developing staffed help lines or advice lines which allow employees to ask for advice or raise concerns without the potential stigma of using a communications resource viewed solely as a vehicle for complaints or accusations. Companies find that such help lines are effective at preventing misconduct rather than simply identifying it after it has taken place. Stakeholders need to know that if they raise an ethical issue, they will be protected against retaliation.
- *Conduct in-house ethics seminars and PBSC workshops*—design a comprehensive program of ethics training that enables employees to become active participants in the learning process.
- Execute the TPS Life Cycle Scan (see Appendix II) *to ensure personnel compliance on at least an annual basis. This* performance excellence model will guide you in this process of continuous business ethics improvement.
- *Penalize unethical behavior*—introduce enforcement procedures, including discipline and dismissal for violations. Let employees know how many others have been disciplined or terminated in a given year over ethical offenses.
- *Show transparency and accountability*—regularly publish detailed reports on own citizenship/sustainability performance, including specific ethics initiatives.
- *Give recognition and reward ethical behavior*—build incentives for ethical behavior into compensation systems, for example, a bonus for ethical performance.
- *Rotate promising managers though the ethics function, grounding them in ethical values as they move toward leadership roles.*
- *Pay special attention to personal ethical values in the personal ambition of candidates in recruiting and hiring practices.*
- *Act as a role model.*

The boxed text below shows a leadership practice, which is an illustrative example in the area of corporate social responsibility.

Leadership Example

Texas Instruments

Texas Instruments (TI) is recognized for having developed a strong ethics program that is actively communicated to all employees. TI's code of ethics was first written in 1961 and has been periodically updated since. A brochure entitled .TI Values and Ethics. serves as TI's basic ethics infrastructure. The brochure was most recently updated in 1998, when the company moved from a rules-based ethics approach to an approach centered more firmly on values. At that time, many of the existing policies and procedures were eliminated in favor of statements based on the company's core values of innovation, integrity and commitment. While the code serves as the foundation for the ethics program, TI's Ethics Office has strengthened it by developing a strong support structure and a number of tools to help employees make ethical decisions. Brochures addressing a range of ethical issues (including topics like working with competitors, working globally, working with suppliers, product safety, business intelligence, workplace safety, and the networked society) have been widely distributed to employees. These brochures describe real-life situations, address the possibility of improper behavior, and provide guidelines on how to make appropriate decisions and list resources available for help. Every new employee receives ethics training, and the company plans to create web-based training for all its employees, tailored to suit each department. The company also provides an intranet ethics website that provides immediate on-line access to key policies, subject-matter contacts, and all printed material and supporting resources. A seven-point Quick Test is used to help guide employees through ethical dilemmas. The Ethics Office has set up an anonymous e-mail system and a 24-hour toll free line for feedback and reporting of issues.

Source: Business for Social Responsibility (BSR, 2005).

Business ethics should not only be based on formal regulations and exhaustive guidelines, but on actual practices. As demonstrated by Enron and others, ethics programs provide no protection from potentially catastrophic ethical failures. Business ethics starts with personal integrity. It must be an informal self-learning process, a way of life based on the continuous balance between personal ambition and personal behavior and the continuous balance between the personal ambition and shared ambition. Ethics programs can be strengthened by stimulating management and employees to act in accordance with their personal principles and values, as formulated in the PBSC. They should implement their personal ambition in accordance with the Plan-Do-Act-Challenge cycle, and on this basis continuously take up ethical challenges. This ethical thinking should be promoted and communicated within the whole company. In this way ethical behavior will become a routine in the organization. Leaders and employees will gain more understanding about their responsibility with regard to ethical behavior. They will understand that it is their responsibility to act ethically, on duty as well as off-duty. This is a more sustainable, comprehensive and holistic approach to ethics and social responsibility.

The informal and voluntary ambition meeting between the line-manager and employee described earlier is an excellent opportunity to promote such behavior. One of the questions in this meeting is—Do you have ethical problems on the job? Miller, et. al. (1996) introduced a way to deal with this issue—

1. Make sure there really is a conflict. Make sure both you and your manager have all the facts. Check the contract to see if the activity is permitted.
2. Determine how much you are likely to risk. Do a cost-benefit analysis. Look at everyone involved, and ask your self what the harm and benefit is to each group.
3. Make your move. If the unethical action is important enough for you to take a risk, tell your manager you cannot do it. Do not be accusatory with your manager. Let him/her save face.
4. If there is trouble, get help. If your manager says you have to do it anyway and you feel that you cannot, then you should go to some influential person in the company. Try not to go directly above your manager's head (i.e. take a 'whistleblower' approach), except as a last resort.
5. Consider a job change. If the people you turn to for help do not have a problem with the situation, then perhaps you need to quit. Evaluate your manager's personal ambition and the shared organizational ambition. If they conflict with yours, then leaving may be the best answer.

The PBSC offers a systemic, sustainable, and integrated approach to strengthen ethics programs within organizations. It helps managers and employees to formulate and understand their company's ethics code and the values that support that code. This process starts at a strategic level, and should be rolled out at the lower levels of the organization. This will be discussed in the next chapter.

CHAPTER 7

ROLLING OUT THE BALANCED SCORECARDS

We are all spiritual beings, composed of minds, bodies, and a spiritual side. To unleash the whole capacity of the individual—mind, body, and spirit—gives enormous power to the organization. It truly empowers members of the organization to devote their entire beings to the ultimate purpose for which the organization exists, which is to erve others.

—Bill George, Former Chairman and CEO, Medtronic Inc.

To be able to convert the strategic vision of an organization into action, it is necessary to link the corporate scorecard (OBSC) to the BSC of departments and teams, as well as the individual performance plan of managers and the employees at lower levels of the organization. Every participant in this process formulates his/her own Personal Balanced Scorecard (PBSC). The ambition meeting between the line-manager and his/her employees takes place at every organizational level. One needs to reflect about the match between one's own personal ambition and the shared ambition at each organizational level. It is important to know which specific inner needs hide behind the behavior of people at each stratum, and what motivates them to stay in the job or leave. Figure 7.1 illustrates the different cascading layers of this process. Each business unit or department sets up its own specific scorecard (which is attuned to the OBSC), as a team under the guidance of the department manager. Each team develops a team

Personal Balanced Scorecard, pages 123–127

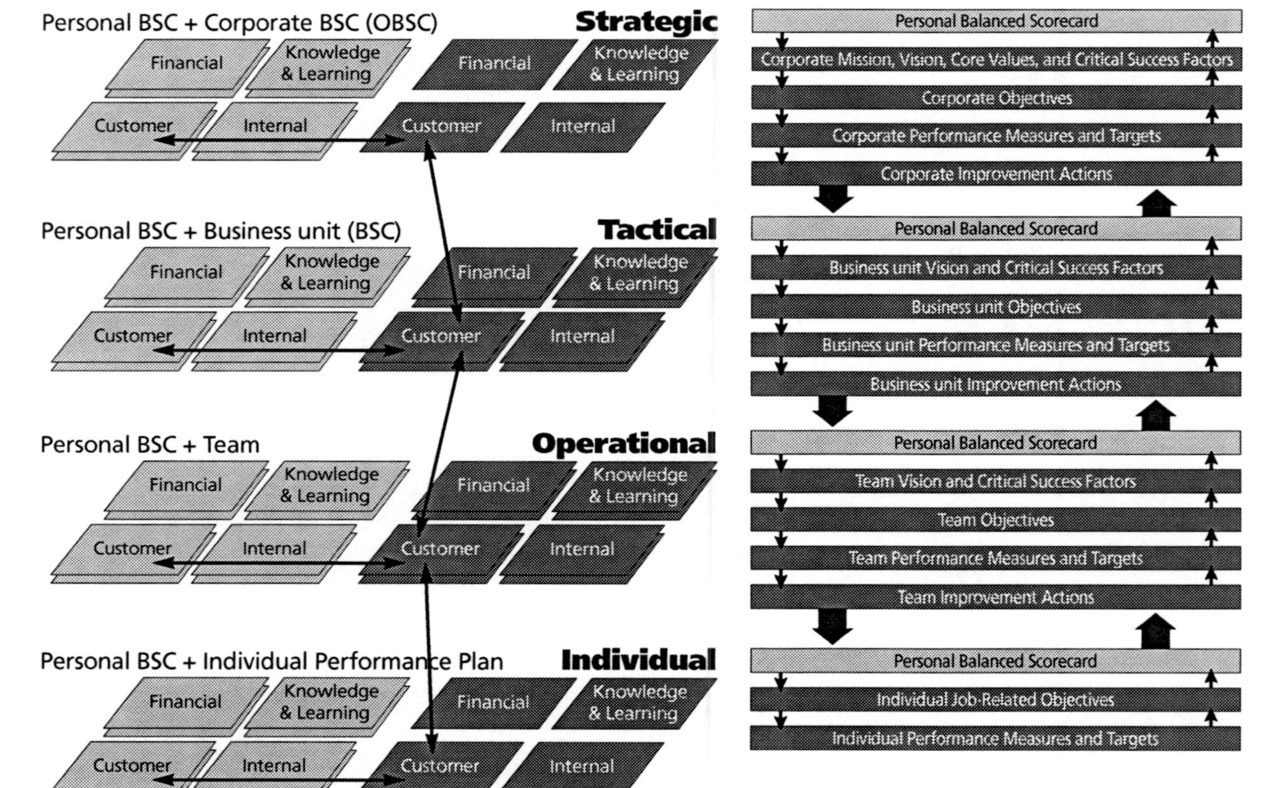

Figure 7.1. Linking the OBSC to the Business Units. Scorecard, Team Scorecard, and Individual Performance Plan (Rampersad, 2003)

scorecard based on the scorecard of its business unit. Then, with the help of the team leader, each team member translates the team scorecard into his or her own individual performance plan, which concentrates on the individual's job. When the objectives are linked in this way, local efforts are aligned with the overall organizational strategy. Brainstorming in several workshops allows the employees to gain better insight into the organizational course that is to be followed. This formulation process is identical for the strategic, tactical, and operational levels within the organization.

The organizational mission formulated in the OBSC applies to all organizational levels. The organizational vision and linked critical success factors, objectives, targets, and improvement actions are then adjusted and fine-tuned to each of the business units and teams. Here, the OBSC is used as a frame of reference. Members of each successively lower level should also reflect on the alignment between their personal ambition and the shared organizational, business unit, and team ambition. The organizational objectives in the OBSC form the point of departure while linking the OBSC to the scorecards at lower organizational levels. For each objective, it is determined whether a given business unit influences this objective significantly, and if improvement actions can be formulated to directly influence its accomplishment. If so, the objective will be incorporated into the scorecard of that business unit. To finalize the business unit's scorecard, the remaining objectives and scorecard elements are formulated, based on the strategy of the business unit. This top-down and bottom-up process is executed iteratively in increasing detail at all organizational levels. In this manner, the overall organizational strategy is systematically translated into more specific plans at each organizational level.

The level of detail with which the translation takes place depends on the organizational typology and the business size. Each department selects those objectives and performance measures from the OBSC that it influences, and then translates them into its own situation. After this process, team scorecards are formulated that are in keeping with the business unit's scorecard. Then, the team scorecard is translated into the individual performance plans of the employees, which focus on the employees' jobs individually. This plan, together with the competence profile of the individual worker and the ambition talk, form the starting point for the effective management of talent within the organization.

Although the Personal Balanced Scorecard and the individual performance plan are strongly interrelated, there are significant differences between them. With the Personal Balanced Scorecard, the emphasis is on the personal life of people, their attitudes, skills, and behavior in society (at work as well as in private life). The individual performance plan, on the other hand, is formulated at the operational level and focuses on the job to be done by the employee within the organization and the improvement of the daily work-related performances. This plan is linked to the team scorecard. As a result of this policy deployment, it is logical to link the individual performance plan explicitly to the reward system as well, without losing track of intrinsic incentive compensation. Several organizations have linked part of their incentive compensation to the financial objectives in the OBSC and the remainder to the objectives related to the external, internal, and knowledge & learning perspectives, depending on the employees' reaching or exceeding related targets. By giving different objectives different weights (priority numbers), unbalanced performances can be prevented. It would be too much to go into further detail about this in the framework of this book. For further information about the individual performance plan, you may consult my book *Total Performance Scorecard* (Rampersad, 2003).

The linked scorecard framework consists of the following four levels (see Figure 7.1)—

1. **Strategic**—All senior management team members first formulate their own PBSCs and share these with their colleagues, in order to promote team learning and mutual trust and respect. The chairman or CEO acts in this process as a trusted person of the other board members. An external senior consultant functions as facilitator and trusted person of the chairman or the CEO. Then, as a team, the corporate mission, vision, critical success factors, core values, objectives, performance measures, targets and improvement actions (the OBSC) are formulated. Subsequently, the chairman or the CEO holds a periodical, informal, voluntary and confidential ambition meeting with his/her board members, in order to align their personal ambition (personal BSC) with the shared corporate ambition (corporate BSC).
2. **Tactical**—The business unit manager (middle manager) shares his or her PBSC with the team leaders, functions as their trusted person for the formulation of their PBSCs and stimulates them to share their PBSCs with each other. This in turn gives rise to team learning and mutual trust and respect within his/her business unit. Then, as a team, the business unit manager and his or her team leaders formulate the vision, critical success factors, objectives, performance measures, targets and improvement actions of his or her business unit (business unit BSC). Following this, the business unit manager holds a periodical, informal, voluntary and confidential ambition meeting with his/her team leaders in order to align their personal ambition (personal BSC) with the shared business unit ambition (business unit BSC). Every business unit does the same.

3. **Operational**—The team leader shares his or her PBSC with his or her team members, functions as their trusted person in formulating their PBSCs and stimulates them to share their PBSCs with each other in order to enhance team learning and mutual trust and respect within his/her team. After this, as a team, the team leader and his/her team members formulate their vision, critical success factors, objectives, performance measures, targets and improvement actions of the team (team BSC). Then, the team leader holds a periodical, informal, voluntary and confidential ambition meeting with the team members in order to align their personal ambition (personal BSC) with the shared team ambition (team BSC). Every team within the business units does the same.
4. **Individual**—The team leader formulates with each of the team members their individual performance plan. This plan consists of the job-oriented objectives, performance measures, and targets of each team member which agree with the team BSC, and with which the team member can identify (the individual performance plan will be discussed further in the next chapter). To facilitate a good match between personal ambition and team ambition, it is recommended that some elements of his/her PBSC will be brought into the individual performance plan of the team member. This can only take place if the team member is receptive. This must be done in consultation with each other.

To illustrate the above mentioned, the linking of the corporate scorecard of Business Jet to the underlying organizational units is given in Table 7.1. The shared ambition of Business Jet was discussed in Chapter 5. The complete BSC of this airliner can be found in my book *Total Performance Scorecard* (Rampersad, 2003). Table 7.1 shows how the scorecard elements of the Safety department of this company are rolled out into the objectives, performance measures, and targets of the Security team as well as the to the related individual performance plan of team member John, regarding Financial perspective only. Each year, the team members formulate their individual performance plan in consultation with the team leader. This plan and the job-related competencies are essential at the periodic result planning, coaching, and appraisal meetings (see next Chapter).

In the next chapter, I will describe how you can integrate the PBSC, OBSC and ambition meeting in the talent development process, and create effective talent management.

Table 7.1. Rollout of the Corporate Scorecard of Business Jet to the Scorecard of Safety Department, Security Team, as Well as to the Related Individual Performance Plan of Team Member John, Regarding Financial Perspective Only

	Organizational Unit	*Objectives*	*Performance Measures*	*Targets*
Financial	*Safety Department*	• Cost control	• Operational costs • % of deviation from department budget	• 13% reduction per end 2007 • Maximum 10% per year
	Security Team	• Lower labor costs • Lower housing costs • Finalizing failure costs study	• Labor costs • $Costs/m^2$ • Failure costs	• 10% reduction in 2 years • 10% reduction as of August 2007 • 40% reduction in 16 months
	Individual (John)	• Working more cost conscience • Implemented cost saving measures • Contribution to failure costs study	• Efficiency • Number of implemented measures • Number of developed improvement proposals	• Increase of 10% in 2007 • At least 2 per quarter • Increase of 30% in 2007

CHAPTER 8

EFFECTIVE TALENT MANAGEMENT

Youth is not a time of life; it is a state of mind. People grow old only by deserting their ideals and by outgrowing the consciousness of youth. Years wrinkle the skin, but to give up enthusiasm wrinkles the soul ... You are as old as your doubt, your fear, and your despair. The way to keep young is to keep your faith young. Keep your self-confidence young. Keep your hope young.

—L.F. Phelan

To be able to manage and utilize the talents within an organization effectively and to create human capital, it is necessary to embed the personal and organizational balanced scorecard as well as the ambition meeting in the talent development process. Figure 8.1 shows how the PBSC concepts create a foundation for effective talent management.

It is recommended to focus on only the voluntary, informal and confidential ambition meeting and the formal progression meetings in the framework of the annual appraisal assessment. In practice, it has been seen that other regular appraisal meetings are often not effective and only divert energy from the real talent development process. It is therefore better to do away with them. Figure 8.2 shows the new talent management model which is being introduced here. The left side of this model includes the individual personal coaching route or individual learning, which consists of the formulation and implementation of the PBSC (aimed at personal effectiveness),

Personal Balanced Scorecard, pages 129–152

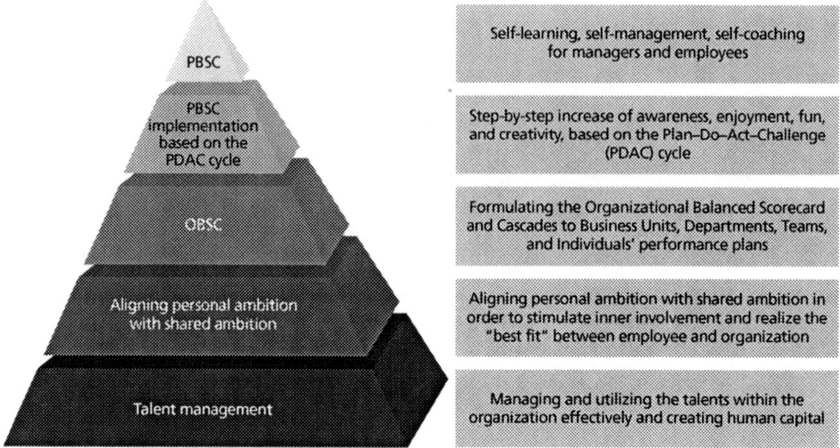

Figure 8.1. PBSC Concept Creates a Foundation For Effective Talent Management

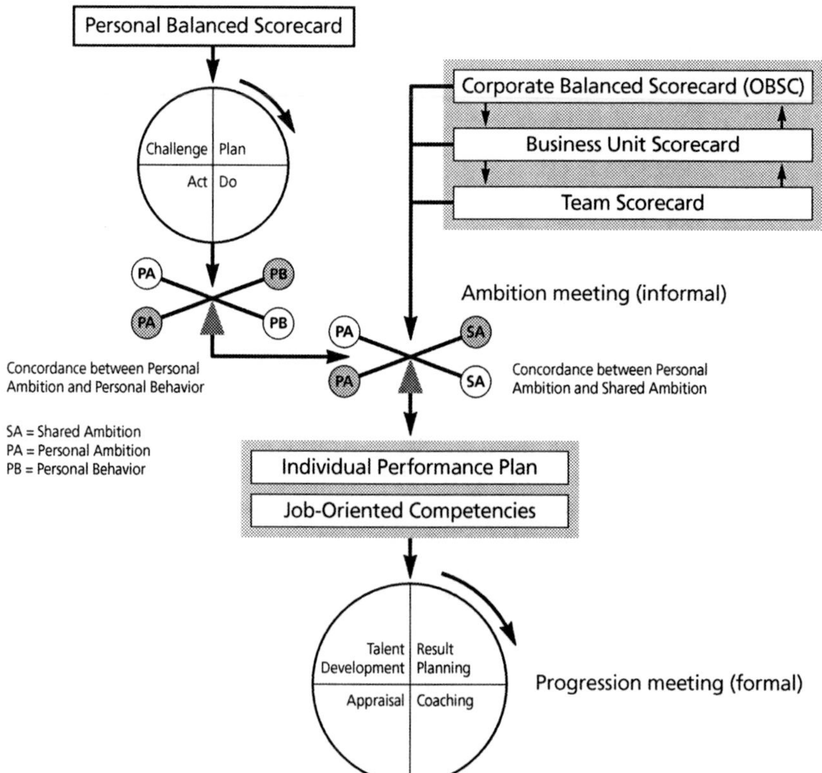

Figure 8.2. Talent Management Model (© Hubert Rampersad)

including the first alignment step (aimed at integrity and ethical behavior). The right side of the model shows the shared ambition or collective learning on the basis of the OBSC. The left and right side come together at the second balance step, which is aimed at employees' inner involvement, motivation, and happiness through the informal and voluntary ambition meeting between the line-manager and his/her employees. Informal coaching is central here. By integrating the left side you will make your organization more human and give it more warmth. The integration of the left side is currently the missing link in management. Further, the left and right side, as well as the second balance step form the input for the formal talent development process. Three roles can be distinguished in this process—

1. The employee, whose responsibility is to continuously develop and improve himself on the basis of his/her PBSC and the Plan-Do-Act-Challenge cycle;
2. The line-manager who, on the one hand, functions as trusted person and informal coach during the ambition meeting on the basis of the employee's PBSC, and, on the other, acts as a formal coach in the execution of the talent development process.
3. The human resources officer, who facilitates the execution of the talent development process (facilitator). A human resources officer on the shop floor is not needed anymore when working according to the PBSC concept.

The formal talent development process consists of—

1. Formulation of the individual performance plan; this entails a summary of the required results (objectives, performance indicators and targets) pertaining to the employee's function about which periodical result agreements are made.
2. Defining a set of job-oriented competencies (inclusive of successive gradations for each competency), which an individual worker must possess to enable him to realize the organizational ambition.
3. Helping employees develop their job-oriented competencies and, as such, improve their functioning. This happens in accordance with the four phases of the introduced talent development cycle (see Figure 8.3)—
    - *Result Planning.* This phase deals with the creation of result agreements based on job-oriented performance objectives in the individual performance plan and the selection of a set of job-oriented competencies, which support these objectives. The individual performance plan is prepared in collaboration with the line-manager. Based on this plan and the set of competencies, peri-

odic result agreements are made between the line-manager and employee regarding the employee's performance and realization of development objectives. In this planning meeting, result agreements are made about the use of selected competencies also. It is recommended to include some job-related elements from the employee's PBSC in the result agreement. This will aid the match between personal ambition and shared ambition, and increase the employee's motivation and commitment.

- *Coaching.* In this phase, the line-manager and employee get together at fixed intervals to discuss the employee's progress; individual guidance occurs, agreements are tested and adjusted, and feedback is given.
- *Appraisal.* The formal appraisal takes place after a certain period to confirm whether all agreements were met, if the agreed results were achieved, and if so, how this was done.
- *Talent Development.* This phase involves the talent development of employees through, for example, courses and on-the-job training, the creation of practice situations, accompanying experienced colleagues, customer feedback meetings, traineeship, development tips, and execution of talent development programs. These are all focused on or related to the employee's own work situation.

Figure 8.3. Talent Development Cycle (© Hubert Rampersad)

Supporting the individual talent development cycle is an organizational talent development practice consisting of a map of competencies for every position and a view of individual capabilities in existing roles. Sophisticated talent management techniques allow positions elsewhere in the organization to be identified and planned for availability to the individual requesting new challenges building on existing capabilities. These moves go beyond functional boundaries and are characteristics of flat, networked organizational designs enabling the organizational to optimize capability and provide optimal individual growth.

By systematically unfolding the above mentioned activities, the job-oriented talent development of the employees can be guided and managed. By way of this gradual development, the employee's self-efficacy increases, the quality of work improves and optimum use is made of his/her abilities, so that the required organizational performances can occur. *Result planning, coaching, appraisal and talent development* are continuously executed in this cyclical process. Many organizations approach talent development in the wrong way; there is often no explicit relationship between individual employee aspirations and the shared ambition; personal development plans are vague and ethical behavior barely gets attention in the process. There is no place for ambition meetings since there is a lack of trust between line-manager and employee, and the private life of employees is systematically ignored. These conditions do not stimulate real learning. I will now briefly discuss the remaining elements of the talent management model (see Figure 8.2). For greater detail, I refer you to my book *Total Performance Scorecard; Redefining Management to Achieve Performance with Integrity* (Rampersad, 2003).

INDIVIDUAL PERFORMANCE PLAN

The individual performance plan is derived from the team scorecard. In this plan, managers and employees together indicate which job-oriented performance objectives the employee is expected to fulfill during the coming period. The joint preparation of this plan has a positive effect on the employee's motivation. It promotes self-guidance since the employee can influence his/her result achievements. The employee's role in this process is to work with his/her line-manager to create the individual performance plan, and to take personal responsibility for his/her own development. The individual performance plan has almost the same construction as the OBSC, with job-oriented objectives, performance measures, and targets that are divided across the 4 result areas (financial, external, internal, and knowledge & learning). These are the essential areas derived from the OBSC, on which employees should focus so as to realize their job objectives. The employee's performance objectives should be formulated in such a way that they are challenging, feasible, specific, measurable, realistic, acceptable, and time bound. It seems obvious (although it is often overlooked) that these objectives must also be agreed upon by both parties, and not directed. The emphasis of the individual performance plan focuses on the results to be obtained instead of, as often happens, the tasks to be executed. When formulating the individual performance plan, be sure to—

- Include job-related elements of employee's PBSC and of the department/team BSC in the individual performance plan (see Figure 8.4)
- Tie the performance objectives to the team BSC
- Gain the employee's understanding and acceptance on each objective, measure, and target
- Set the performance objectives jointly—this can be revised if the situation changes
- Set a manageable number of objectives; too many objectives will result in lack of focus
- Set checkpoints and milestones to review progress on the objectives and agree up front on the criteria for the achievement of these objectives
- Discuss the related competencies the employee will need to demonstrate in order to achieve the objectives

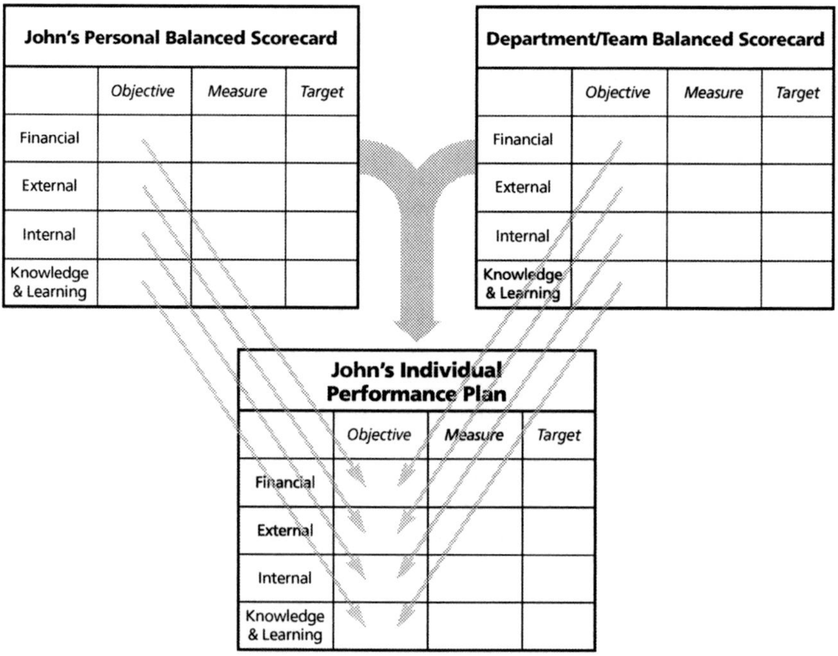

John's Personal Balanced Scorecard

	Objective	Measure	Target
Financial			
External			
Internal			
Knowledge & Learning			

Department/Team Balanced Scorecard

	Objective	Measure	Target
Financial			
External			
Internal			
Knowledge & Learning			

John's Individual Performance Plan

	Objective	Measure	Target
Financial			
External			
Internal			
Knowledge & Learning			

Figure 8.4. Where the OBSC meets the PBSC

To illustrate this process, I present the individual performance plan of John (security team leader of Business Jet) in Table 8.1. The scorecard of his team was discussed in Chapter 7. The complete BSC of Business Jet, including the complete roll out into the objectives, performance measures and targets on lower levels organizational levels, can be found in my book *Total Performance Scorecard; Redefining Management to Achieve Performance with Integrity* (Rampersad, 2003). John formulated his individual performance plan in consultation with his team leader. This plan and the job-oriented competencies are being used during the periodic result planning, coaching, and appraisal meetings. The job-oriented competencies will be discussed in the next section.

JOB-ORIENTED COMPETENCIES

A job-oriented competency is an ability, behavior or skill that has been shown to cause or predict outstanding performance in a given job. Job-oriented competencies may be categorized as—

- *Competencies related to the job and level of thinking*
- *Knowledge competencies*—what he or she must learn and know
- *Skill competencies*—what he or she must be able to do
- *Behavioral competencies*—attitudes, principles, norms and values, demeanor, and the driving forces needed to hold the position

Competencies help employees understand how they are expected to achieve better results and they help manager to coach the employees. Each competency consists of a clear definition and a description of specific, observable behaviors. Examples of job oriented competencies are—effective communication, innovation, taking initiatives, coaching, effective delegation, proactive behavior, inspirational ability, persuasion, and so on. For the effective fulfillment of one's job, one should have different competencies at one's disposal. The number of organizational competencies differs for each job, and depends primarily on the nature and complexity of the job. It is important to be realistic and not exaggerate the number of competencies required. Let the line-manager and his/her employee select five to eight competencies that are most relevant to the job. The following questions may be useful for this purpose—

- Which are the critical tasks within a function related to the shared ambition?
- What knowledge and skills should the worker possess to enable him to perform his/her tasks adequately?
- What scope of thinking is required?
- Which attitudes or behaviors are expected of him/her?

Table 8.1. John's Individual Performance Plan

	Objectives	Performance Measures	Targets
	Individual Performance Plan		
	Organization: Business Jet **Department:** Safety **Manager:** Steve		
	Employee: John **Job:** Team Leader **Team:** Security Team **Period:** Jan. 2007–Dec. 2007		
Financial	• Working more cost consciously	• Efficiency	• Increase of 10 % in 2007
	• Implemented cost saving measures	• Number of implemented measures	• At least two a quarter
	• Contribution to failure costs study	• Number of developed improvement proposals	• Increase of 30 % in 2007
External	• Customer friendly behavior while executing security tasks	• Number of passenger complaints	• Decrease of at least 50 % this year
	• Improved satisfaction level from my customers about my behavior	• Satisfaction score of customers	• Listen better to my customers and respect them.
Internal	• Contribution provided to risk analysis	• Number of developed safety suggestions	• Minimal 2 quarterly
	• Less serious mistakes made during execution security tasks	• Number of serious mistakes	• Decrease of 50 % by the year's end
	• Physical and mental health	• % of Sick leave	• Decrease of less than 2 % by no later than November 2007
		• % of Stress	• Decrease of at least 30 % by the end of 2007
	• Effective coaching of team members	• % of Employees who think they are coached effectively	• 75% in June 2007
K&L	• Improved Competences in the field of Safety	• Safety certificate	• 30% of certificates obtained in July 2007
	• Active participation in improvement teams	• Number of solved safety problems	• 75% by the end of 2007
	• Improved coaching skills	• Satisfaction degree of team members regarding way of coaching	• Minimum of 75% by the end of 2007

The selected competencies are assessed on a separate form during the coaching and appraisal meeting by awarding scores for each. To register these scores, point scales with two to five levels and with various descriptions are used. After defining the selected competencies the required behaviors of each competency need to be described in four to five gradations, where the behavior regarding the competency in question is described in various ways. At the end of the appraisal period, the line-manager addresses the levels of each competency, based on the observed performance. A rating for each competency is agreed upon, which then gives an overall rating.

RESULT PLANNING

Agreements are made in the result planning meeting between the line-manager and employee regarding the result areas, objectives, performance measures, and targets on the one hand, and the use of job-oriented competencies for adequate job fulfillment, on the other. During this result planning meeting, pertinent opinions and arguments are exchanged, expectations are expressed, and it is determined what the employee will do to achieve results and to comply with the agreed job demands. Here, the employee will also indicate if this is feasible, what he/she thinks can or cannot be realized, what his/her personal ambitions and aspirations are, what he/she will need in order to achieve these results, and what the possible barriers to this might be. When conducting the result planning meeting, be sure to—

- Conduct a two-way discussion (not a lecture);
- Establish a positive tone and climate for this meeting;
- Listen to the employee's viewpoints;
- Encourage an open dialogue and get the employee involved;
- Listen to the employee's reaction and perceptions;
- Pay attention to the employee's PBSC, including his/her support in private life.

As mentioned previously, it is recommended to include some elements from the employee's PBSC in the result agreements as well (if he is receptive), so as to stimulate his/her inner involvement, motivation and dedication and to realize the "best fit" between personal ambition and the shared ambition. On the result agreement forms, the following aspects are documented—

- name, occupation, and signature of the employee and that of his/her manager
- the agreement period
- the result areas

- five to eight related agreements (including, for each agreement, its relative importance, one or more objectives, and the matching performance measures and targets)
- the manager's support for the achievement of the agreed results
- and the dates of the planning, coaching, and appraisal meetings

The agreements regarding the behaviors (competencies) supporting the results to be obtained are frequently written on a separate form. For each competency, the following aspects are documented—definition; levels and their relative importance; the expected behaviors of the employee during the coming appraisal period; and the support to be given by the line-manager when the relevant competencies are used. The manager and employee each receive a copy of the completed forms; the original is filed in the personnel dossier.

COACHING

During the second phase of the talent development cycle (see Figure 8.3), the manager helps the employee achieve the results agreed upon earlier and helps initiate the competencies discussed. This regards formal coaching, as part of the progression meetings (see Figure 8.2). Two to three times a year, the manager will conduct an open and two-sided progress meeting with the employee. Based on the copy of the completed planning forms, the progress and the agreements made with respect to performance and development of the employee's objectives are evaluated, tested, and adjusted if required. Coaching occurs here in order to help improve job quality, develop the talents of the employee (long-term as well as short-term), improve the way he/she works, and have a positive influence on his/her motivation. Coaching also includes providing new challenges and ongoing information to employees about their performance, giving recognition to encourage and to reward good performance, etc. Providing guidance and recognition frequently when it has been earned builds an employee's self-efficacy or confidence and self-esteem. In the coaching phase, formal interim reviews of the employee's progress also take place, assessing the employee's strengths and areas for further development. In this phase, the manager works as a *formal coach.* The line-manager functions, however, as a trusted person at the ambition meeting (i.e. as an *informal coach*), a voluntary process with the employee's PBSC as a guideline. The manager and his/her employee keep the reports of the formal coaching meeting, until all agreements have been realized.

The first coaching meeting deserves special attention. The objectives, rules, methods, and frequency of coaching must be clear to everyone. In the coaching section of the appraisal form, the following points are mentioned—what is going well, what can be done better, how can it be done better, which obstacles have been encountered, which situational factors have influenced the completion of the job, which training must be provided, and how. The questions that are central here are—how is it going? How can it be done better? What motivates you? What discourages you? Does everyone abide by the agreements made? Are the behaviors displayed sufficient to achieve the results? Where does the job constantly go wrong? What have you learned? What have you unlearned? Agreements are also made for the period up to the appraisal (who does what and when?). It is also of importance to know why co-workers don't do what is expected of them. Various reasons can be mentioned, such as, they don't know what they are supposed to do or, how to do it and why they should do it; they think your way will not work, their way is better, they are already doing it, or something else is more important. Effective coaching by the manager is essential here.

Robert Greenleaf wrote—*"Good leaders must first become good servants"*

Klaus Schwab, Founder and Chairman of the World Economic Forum, believed that

> The three dimensions of leadership are Mind, Heart and Soul, as follows—
>
> 1. Mind connotes the professionalism necessary to master expertise and lead a field, as well as the measure of respect merited by and accorded to consummate professionals. Great leaders command such respect.
> 2. Heart connotes the passionate engagement with cause, duty and service, as well as the emotion of love awakened in a following, which is attracted to and energized by intensity of passion. Great leaders engender such love.
> 3. Soul connotes the commitment to a mission and the values necessary to fulfill it, as well as the trust earned through navigating by a moral compass (as opposed to an expedient radar screen). Great leaders inspire such fidelity.

Also remember what N. R. Narayana Murthy, Chairman of Infosys Technologies Limited, said: *"The trust of employees is the most important ingredient for successful leadership."*

Table 8.2 shows a list of attitude, tasks and skills of effective leaders and coaches.

Table 8.2. Attitudes, Tasks and Skills of Effective Leaders and Coaches (Rampersad, 2003)

Attitudes and Tasks	*Skills*
• Considers his/her employees as human beings more than as employees	• Has a high degree of self- awareness, self-regulation and empathy.
• Stimulates a fundamental learning attitude and working smarter instead of harder	• Is open, honest, trustworthy, and consistent, without a hidden agenda

Table 8.2. Attitudes, Tasks and Skills of Effective Leaders and Coaches (Rampersad, 2003) (Cont.)

Attitudes and Tasks	*Skills*
• Pays attention to own and employee's spiritual development • Relies on his/her intuitions • Knows and understands employee's personal ambition, life circumstances, strengths, habits, weaknesses, problems, feelings towards the work, likes and dislikes • Teaches the employee how to learn and encourages him/her to share knowledge with colleagues • Does not hide or try to get around problems • Gives the employee the recognition due and shows appreciation for contributions • Listens actively to the employee and respects him/her • Lets the employee keep self-esteem and respect, and support his/her skills • Helps the employee take on responsibilities and encourages employee independence • Is a sounding board and continuously focused on developing and mobilizing knowledge • Lays down the boundaries where the employee can make independent decisions • Keeps appointments and shows the drive to obtain results • Supplies the employee with a feeling of safety • Builds trust and respect, and cherishes them • Shows vision and propagates this decisively • Shows involvement, gives the employee space but is visible • Stimulates teamwork, based on mutual respect, openness, and mutual trust • Creates a climate of enjoyment, passion, devotion, and enthusiasm • Allows arguments to influence his/her decision making	• Is unselfish and a servant • Has no ego • Has self-knowledge based on his/her PBSC • Has intuitive abilities • Is patient, decisive, positive, enthusiastic, proactive, result-oriented and open to change • Has perseverance and power of persuasion • Has the ability to bring out the hidden possibilities of the employee • Thinks conceptually without losing contact with reality • Knows how to get the best out of the employee • Listens well • Can place him/herself in the position of the employee • Is serviceable and modest • Can carry out norms and values so that a "we feeling" develops • Can convince the employee that the chosen way is the right one • Can build a confidential relationship • Can handle constructive confrontation • Can distinguish the important from the less important and can balance short- and long-term priorities well • Can communicate clearly, openly, and at the right time • Can solve problems systematically and structurally • Has the talent to identify notable trends and anticipate them ahead of time • Can activate, motivate, and stimulate people • Has the ability to decide where the organization should go and distinguish between dreams and hard facts

Table 8.2. Attitudes, Tasks and Skills of Effective Leaders and Coaches (Rampersad, 2003) (Cont.)

Attitudes and Tasks	*Skills*
• Is accessible to the employee, inspires him/her and gives constructive feedback • Shows the employee how his/her activities contribute to the greater whole • Inspires the employee to set concrete, practical, and measurable goals, and to accomplish them • Stimulates and motivates the employee to take initiatives and serve the customer • Maintains and stimulates the relationships with the employee with understanding • Creates circumstances in which the employee is successful and where he/she is responsible for his/her work • Stimulates individual and team learning, and inspires intensive knowledge exchange • Allows mistakes • Stimulates informal contacts between employees • Creates transparency in tasks and positions • Helps employees to distinguish between main and secondary issues and gives a helping hand when needed • Takes personal circumstances and employee's private life into account • Ensures work-life balance • Praises employees who perform well, and pays attention to those with shortcomings • Preferably communicates face-to-face • Believes in him/herself and others • Has formulated his/her PBSC and applied this in work and life according to the PDAC cycle • Shares own PBSC with employees • Conducts periodical ambition meetings with his/her employees • Strives for the "best fit" between employee's personal ambition and shared ambition • Stimulates employees to formulate and apply their PBSC and share this with each other	• Is innovative and dares to accept mistakes • Gives direction but is open for the input of others • Can motivate, inspire, and make people enthusiastic • Is open and flexible but can at the same time take strong action • Can create involvement and cultivate a culture of participation • Can avoid conflicts and negotiates well • Can adequately asses the talents and shortcomings of employees

The manager, in addition to this, must discuss the performance gap in a non-judgmental way and give performance feedback. Performance feedback is essential for formal coaching. I have explained this in detail in the boxed text that follows.

Giving and Receiving Performance Feedback (Rampersad, 2005)

Providing performance feedback involves giving employees constructive feedback on performance that needs to be improved. It identifies what needs to be improved, why this is important, and how to improve. Giving and receiving performance feedback involves redirecting, correcting, and complimenting.

Some general guidelines. Performance feedback:

- Describes the behavior and performance that has led to the feedback; it does not make a description about the employee.
- Is not given to judge the employee, it is just something that is mentioned in order to achieve improvement.
- Is specific, rather than general; it is clear so that the employee understands its message. It should be focused on important rather than trivial issues.
- Is focused on improving for the future, rather than blaming for the past.
- Is in the interest of both employee and manager.
- Is helpful, rather than destructive.
- Is developmental, rather than remedial
- Is only meaningful if and when the employee is open to it.
- Should be prompt, rather than delayed.
- Is two-way, rather than one-way.

The most important feedback rules for the *manager* are:

- Clarify to yourself beforehand what you want to say and collect the necessary data.
- Be patient and constructive. Observe performance and give constructive feedback.
- Measure performance results against the objectives. Discuss the performances with the employee and adjust the individual performance plan. Help the employee to adjust his/her PBSC.
- Present the feedback in such a way that it is seen as an opportunity and not a threat.
- Be objective and specific; make clear what effects the employee's performance has had on you and include examples and comments.
- Be open and honest.
- Be complete; take time to make the feedback helpful.
- Make your observation of the other person's behavior descriptive (what you see) and not judgmental (giving assessments).

- Convey what you observe in terms of specific behavior or performance, not personal attacks or generalized judgments.
- Give the employee the opportunity to react; listen intently and keep an open mind to his or her opinion.
- Show that you trust the employee and end the conversation with some positive remarks about the future.
- Appreciate your employees for who they are, not only for their accomplishments.
- Be selective in giving feedback; only give feedback if the employee can benefit from it at this time.

The most important feedback rules for the *employee* are:

- Listen attentively and closely to your manager before you accept the feedback; ask for clarification when something is not clear.
- Don't go into a defensive mode or start attacking; don't look for explanations; performance feedback is a learning process.
- Accept the feedback and analyze why you're acting in the way that has been addressed.
- Know that your manager is kindly disposed towards you; don't feel that you are being attacked.
- Don't express negative feelings; study the feedback with your manager.
- Don't try to be humorous or smart; concentrate on a change for the better. Strive to meet or exceed performance expectations.
- Summarize the feedback to be able to formulate your observations.
- Ask questions to clarify the feedback.
- Carefully evaluate the usefulness of the feedback.
- Don't react vehemently and aggressively towards negative feedback; get information from it.
- Don't consider the feedback to be criticism.
- Show appreciation to your manager because he or she had the courage to help you.
- Document the lessons learned from the feedback.
- Assess your performance against your individual performance plan and your PBSC. Look for opportunities to learn and to improve your performance continuously.

APPRAISAL

Appraisal is the third phase in the development cycle (see Figure 8.3). This takes place during the appraisal meeting at the end of the process. During the appraisal meeting, the forms that were completed during the previous phases of result planning and coaching are discussed. This meeting takes one to two hours and, unlike the coaching meeting, is one-sided. Here the manager alone gives his/her opinion about how the employee is performing. This appraisal is based on an observation of the employee's behavior during the entire period and the realization of the result agreements. The manager checks if all agreements are fulfilled, whether the agreed upon results were obtained according to the targets, and how they were realized. This assessment deals primarily with the results of the measurements. The result and career agreements that have been made are also evaluated. By giving feedback to the employee throughout the year, and by having frequent coaching meetings, the likelihood that the employee will accept the appraisal is positively influenced and surprises are prevented. The manager gives his or her judgment regarding employee performance on the appraisal form, in terms of the result agreement and competency. Based on these two opinions, a final opinion is given. This form also registers the date of the meeting and development needs (education and training to be followed in order to improve employee performance and capability development). The appraisal meeting concludes with an explanation about the opinion as well as the signatures of the manager and the employee. The completed appraisal form is placed in the employee's personnel file, and both the manager and employee receive a copy of it.

The 360°-feedback approach is used more and more frequently within the scope of appraisal and talent development, in order to obtain a more reliable image of employee's behaviors. The 360°-feedback method is an effective form of appraisal and learning, whereby employees not only obtain feedback from their immediate supervisors regarding how they work (behavior and performance), but also from colleagues, subordinates, customers, suppliers, and others who have insight into their daily activities. They function here as providers of feedback and as points of reference by completing an anonymous questionnaire about the employee's job-oriented competencies. This list may also be completed by the employee himself, who is here the feedback receiver. The 360°-feedback system is a valuable supplement to the mixed appraisal system described earlier. It is a method used more frequently at middle management and operational levels to obtain a reliable picture of the employee's and manager's behavior. It is an effective method for learning, improving, and performing.

TALENT DEVELOPMENT

Once the result planning, coaching, and appraisal meetings have been conducted and 360°-feedback obtained, both the employee and manager know which job-oriented competencies should be developed further in order to fulfill the job adequately and professionally. A broad range of instruments can be used for the employee's talent development, such as—

- Traineeship, courses, workshops, conferences, and on-the job training, all focused on the employee's work situation.
- Creation of practice situations, gaining experience through doing (learning by doing).
- Individual guidance and coaching in the workplace;
- Appointment of mentors or coaches for junior workers, and having them accompany experienced colleagues who can pass on experience to them.
- 360°-feedback, job rotation, benchmarking, development tips and team building.
- Learning from one's own strengths and weaknesses (self-reflection) on the basis of the PBSC and anticipation in accordance with the Plan-Do-Act-Challenge cycle.
- Introduction of a periodic, confidential, informal and voluntary ambition meeting between the line-manager and the worker, using the PBSC of the worker as topic.
- Stimulation from the use of the PBSC, focused at work as well as spare time; managers and employees must take the initiative and the responsibility on the basis of the PBSC to keep developing their own talents. They must not blame others for their failures.

In many cases, it is mandatory to follow all these development routes, which are meant to give the employee the opportunity to develop those competencies that are important to the effective fulfillment of his or her job. It is encouraged to develop these competencies as far as possible in practice, through learning by doing and on the job situations.

Remember what John W. Gardner said—*"Much education today is monumentally ineffective. All too often we are giving young people cut flowers when we should be teaching them to grow their own plants."*

Acquiring new insights and skills and integrating them in daily work, result in different behaviors and working smarter (instead of harder). It may be pointed out here that knowledge and skill competencies can be learned. Behavior competencies, on the contrary, are partly innate and, therefore difficult to train. In many cases this can be developed through individual coaching. To benefit effective talent development, it is also suggested to systematically include the employee's PBSC in this process and align it with his or her job-oriented talent development. In addition, encourage employees to bring into practice what they have learned from development efforts and to share their knowledge and experience with colleagues. When they do so, pay them compliments. Ask them in which area they wish to develop their learning possibilities and let them include these in their PBSC and individual performance plan. This can be linked with Gary Jacobs' conception—

See an individual as a whole person and not just in his role as employee.

Try to know and understand his personal ambition, life circumstances, strengths, habits, weaknesses, problems, feelings towards work, likes and dislikes. Treat him according to this knowledge with due respect for his ideas and feelings, desires and needs, interest in his development, concern for his growth, happiness, health and well-being. ...The best means to give attention to employees is to take interest in the work that they do and give just recognition, and in that context to provide each employee with the opportunity to constantly learn new skills and obtain new knowledge and exercise new responsibilities appropriate to his capabilities ...There are a number of criteria to ensure that each man receives the attention he deserves:

1. He should be considered as a human being more than as an employee;
2. The job he does should result in psychological satisfaction making him desire to have more work;
3. He should find constantly newer skills added to his capacity;
4. His work-pattern should include a built-in recreation that prevents accumulation of frustration or tension;
5. His work should help to harness all energies and give them to the work so that tedium, except the physical part, will be minimal;
6. There should be a genuine appreciation and psychological recognition of talents when they are found or freshly emerge. Work must help to reveal and develop these talents".

Based on Accenture's High Performance Workforce Study in North America (December 2004), these remarks were made—

As achieving high performance in companies increasingly hinges on a company's people, effectively boosting the skills and productivity of critical workforces becomes a paramount issue. For most, this means targeting a number of HR and training shortcomings that are preventing workforces from realizing their full potential. By investing strategically in new integrated solutions that address the full life cycle of the employee—including the critical processes of recruiting, learning and performance management—companies can bring a more disciplined, rigorous approach to human resources and learning. In the process, they can create high-performance workforces that can position them for sustained competitive advantage for years to come.

The PBSC concept will help you realize this ambition.

I know one company in which talent management based on the PBSC principles is a way of life. This company is Infosys Technologies Ltd., a world leader in consulting and information technology services and one of the world's fastest growing technology companies. This Indian company has entered its 25th year. The chairman of the board of this IT powerhouse, N. R. Narayana Murthy, plans to make the company a bigger, stronger, and global player. At an analysts' meet in Hyderabad on August 12, 2005, to mark the silver jubilee celebrations of Infosys, Mr. Narayana Murthy spoke about his ambition for the future.

Narayana Murthy's Ambition for the Future

We start our silver jubilee celebrations today. It is indeed laudable that we have run this marathon so far. Several happy thoughts come to my mind as I stand here. The most important relates to when Infosys began. It was a wintry morning in January 1981 when seven of us sat in my apartment, and created Infosys. We had lots of hope, confidence, commitment, energy, enthusiasm, hard work, passion and a sense of sacrifice. We were short of one thing, money. We managed to put together just $250 in seed capital. We never dreamt about size, revenues and profits. Our dream, right from day one, was to build a corporation that was, above all things, respected. From the beginning, our team was unique in our commitment to a strong value system. We believed in putting the interest of the company ahead of our own interest. We believed in a legal and ethical business. We believed in respect and long-term gratification. And each of us brought complementary strengths to the company.

To me, entrepreneurship is a marathon. I believe that the key to a successful corporation is longevity. My heroes are companies like IBM, Levers, and GE. These firms have shown growth in earnings quarter after quarter, for a long time. Infosys itself has seen consistent growth in revenue and profitability for over 49 quarters, since it got listed in India. We have institutionalized performance and accountability in our systems and processes, and through the empowerment of our employees. Let me talk about some of the generic lessons we have learned.

The name of the game is: predictability of revenues; sustainability of the prediction; profitability; and a good de-risking model. Measurement is the key to improvement. A sound value system is what differentiates long-term players from others. Putting the corporation's interest ahead of personal interest will advance personal goals in the long term. No single person is indispensable. It is important that you give challenging engagements to deserving people, whether they are young or new in the organization. Youth and empowerment are the keys to scalability and longevity. Every situation is what you make it to be. Confidence is half the battle, and leadership is making the impossible look possible. Speed, imagination and excellence in execution are the only three context-invariant and time-invariant attributes for success. The trust of employees is the most important ingredient for successful leadership. To gain the trust of people, there is no more powerful leadership style than leadership by example. The world respects performance and action, not rhetoric. It is better to obsolete our own innovations, rather than allowing our competitors to do it. A healthy sense of paranoia and respect for competition is an absolute must for success. It prevents complacency, and ensures that the organization is learning continuously.

The ultimate test for customer satisfaction is making our customer look good in front of his/her customer. I have realized that if you want to look smarter, you must surround yourself with people smarter than you.

Everybody needs incentives to perform. Money is not the only motivator. Respect, dignity, fairness and inclusiveness are essential to get the best out of employees. Every employee must feel an inch taller when talking about the company. Being transaction-oriented in every decision avoids groupism. An emphasis on meritocracy and data-orientation enhances the confidence of employees in the fairness of the corporation. We believe in the adage, In God we trust, everybody else brings data to the table. To retain the trust of your investors, it is better to under promise and over-deliver. Investors understand that every business will have ups and downs, and want us to level with them at all times. They want us give them bad news pro-actively and as early as possible. Therefore, when in doubt, disclose.

We have realized that we should never take any decision with the stock price in mind. The day we do this, we will ruin the company. Finally, we have realized that we can shortchange investors if we want to make Rs 1 crore (Rs 10 million), but if we want to make Rs 1,000 crore (Rs 10 billion), we have to play the game straight and honest. We have realized that longevity requires that we follow every law of the land, even if we do not agree with it. We should work hard to change laws that hurt the progress of the corporation. Unless we make a difference to the society and earn their trust, we cannot be long-term players. Therefore, in everything we do, we must ask ourselves whether we are adding value to the society around us, regardless of where we are, US or India.

"What I want Infosys to achieve in 25 years"? What do I want to see this company achieve in the next 25 years? I want this to be a place where people of different races, nationalities and religious beliefs work together, in an environment of intense competition but utmost courtesy and dignity, to add greater and greater value to our customers, day after day. Just like we have received respect in India, I want Infosys to be the most respected company in every country that it operates. But, to achieve these dreams, we have to be in existence over the next 250 years. I know we can do this for the following reasons:

- We have an extraordinary leader in Nandan (Nandan Nilekani, Infosys CEO), a man of great vision, values and dynamism. He is ably supported by the best management team and professionals in the industry.
- We have a depth of leaders within the organization, with over 500 leaders being part of our leadership training and mentoring programme.
- The de-risking strategy at Infosys ensures that there is a backup for every position, and that decision-making is participatory across the company.
- In other words, it is not one person, but a team that looks at every decision.

Thus, at Infosys, it is the leadership of ideas and meritocracy that drives every decision. Every decision is supported by a strong portfolio of systems, processes and technology. The value system of the company is time and context invariant. We will continue to have the mindset of a small company even as we grow and scale. Finally, and most importantly, I see youth, the feel-good factor and confidence around me. This is why I am confident Infosys will continue to serve society as a long-term player.

Human Resource policies play a vital role in the talent development of employees. Objective recruitment policies and the PBSC method can ensure the necessary job fit by matching the abilities, aptitude and motivation of the employees with the requirements of the jobs and with the shared ambition of the organization. It should be clear from the foregoing that the PBSC could effectively be put into action as a recruiting instrument. The human resources officer, using their formulated personal ambition, will have a better insight into the ambitions and motives of prospective candidates. The personal ambition of a candidate tells a greater story than a resume. It is possible that a candidate seems suitable for a specific function on the basis of his/her CV, but, if there is a poor match between his/her personal ambition and the ambition of the organization, this would not aid his/her performances. A good match between the job description and the personal ambition of the candidate therefore results in higher customer satisfaction. Thus, by using the PBSC method, it is therefore possible to select applicants more effectively and to handle intake meetings more structurally with them. With the PBSC concept, the right candidate can be selected for the right job. The boxed text below shows possible measures for creating high-performance workforces and the effective management of talents within your organization.

Measures for Effective Talent Management

- Provide time to communicate authentically with your employees... not just about work, involve them in decision making whenever possible, show appreciation to each employee frequently and laugh more often.
- Make people happy by letting them control their own actions and lives and face challenges. They will be happiest if they are given freedom. This requires the opportunity to build self-respect, trust, feelings of responsibility, and involvement.
- Empower people; help them to be capable of what they really are capable of.
- Organizations are living organisms, in which people live; treat them

like human beings. If you have a sound business strategy that is based on caring for people and not harming anyone, then financial success will come automatically.

- Train and coach employees continuously to gain new skills that are within their capacity. Assist employees in developing their intuitive skills on the basis of the PBSC approach. To make decision on the basis of intuition is fast, accurate and effective. Choose new employees also on the basis of these skills.
- Stimulate management and employees to formulate their PBSCs themselves, and to implement them in accordance with the Plan-Do-Act-Challenge cycle, and on this basis continuously enter into new challenges. The more innovative an organization needs to be, the more its members need to formulate and implement their PBSCs. Let managers and employees define their specific and measurable personal development objectives on the basis of the PBSC and make them responsible to reach these goals. These must be attuned to their specific learning situation. The personal development objectives and activities must correspond with the Organizational Balanced Scorecard (OBSC).
- Introduce an informal and voluntary ambition meeting between the line-manager and his/her employee.
- Stimulate employees to gain more understanding for self-responsibility and let them understand that their development is their own responsibility. Let them understand that it is their ethical duty and responsibility to develop themselves and become more proactive, for the good of themselves, their loved ones, their work, their organization, their country, and the world.
- Ensure a safe environment in which employees are willing to learn, try out new things, take on new challenges, and develop related skills in accordance with the PDAC cycle.
- Ensure a work-life balance and an enjoyable atmosphere.
- Trust your employees. Ralph Waldo Emerson said: *"Trust men and they will be true to you; treat them greatly and they will show themselves great."*
- Allow mistakes. Give employees the freedom to make failures. Without failures, learning does not exist and taking up challenges is not encouraged. According to Henry Ford: *"Failure is simply the opportunity to begin again, this time more intelligently."* There are no failures, only lessons.
- Give employees self-confidence. Remember what Jack Welch said: *"Giving people self-confidence is by far the most important thing that you can do. Because then they will act."*
- Stimulate management and employees to act ethically while balancing between personal ambition and personal behavior, so that inner peace and personal credibility can be developed. Without ethical action, there is no sustainable individual learning.

- Strive for the .best fit. between employee and organization on the basis of the balance between personal and organizational ambition and, through this, to stimulate pleasure and inner involvement.
- Perform the breathing and silence exercise each morning for 10-20 minutes.
- Introduce a periodic, informal, voluntary and confidential ambition meeting. Help managers use train-the-trainer sessions to enable them to effectively fulfill the role of trusted person and coach.
- Help managers and human resources officers understand that in this process they need to fulfill the role of trusted facilitator. It is their task to improve the quality of life of employees on the basis of the PBSC method and the PDAC cycle, and have them enter into greater challenges and let them enjoy their work and make them happy. Quality of life of customers will also improve and they will be more contented and more satisfied.
- Help managers and human resources officers to understand that a healthy home situation has an important influence at work and this should not be ignored. Their task is also to encourage their employees to systematically apply their PBSC within their family and to help improve the situation at home on the basis of the PDAC cycle.
- Stimulate managers and employees to share their PBSCs with each other in order to create team learning and mutual trust.
- Make a real priority of talent development, and take it up as a challenge.
- Teach managers and employees how to learn. According to Carl Rogers: *"The only person who is educated is the one who has learned how to learn ... and change."*
- Stimulate informal contact between employees.
- Make sure that role models exist.
- Chase away fear and distrust from the organization on the basis of the Total Performance Scorecard and PBSC concept. With no fear, less management intervention, and higher autonomy, work becomes more satisfying.
- Create conditions whereby people are prepared to bring their knowledge into action, to share this with each other and to learn how to learn.
- Promote simplicity of the organizational structure and simplicity of managers. use of language.
- Let employees identify and solve common problems as a team.
- Give top priority to the interests of your staff, second priority to the interests of your customers, and third priority to the interests of your shareholders.
- Organize multi-disciplinary brainstorming sessions, problem-solving meetings, in-company project valuation meetings and speeches with external experts.

- Stimulate trust between line-managers and employees by encouraging line-managers and employees to share their personal ambition with each other.
- Use objective recruitment policies and the PBSC as a recruiting instrument

In the following chapter, I introduce the PBSC cycle, which is meant to be helpful for the implementation of the complete PBSC system.

CHAPTER 9

THE PBSC CYCLE

You are what your deepest nature is. As your nature is, so is your will. As your will is, so is your deed. As your deed is, so is your destiny.

—Brihadaranyaka Upanishad

In this, the final chapter, I introduce the holistic PBSC cycle in which the relationships between the elements of the PBSC system discussed so far are displayed. This holistic and organic model will be helpful for successfully implementing your Personal and Organizational Balanced Scorecards. It consists of the following four phases (see Figure 9.1):

1. **Formulating**—This phase involves the formulation of the Personal and Organizational Balanced Scorecards, including the use of the integrated breathing and silence exercise during this formulation process (see Chapter 2).
2. **Communicating and linking**—Here all stakeholders participate in the business strategy by effectively communicating and translating (rolling out) the corporate scorecard to the scorecards of all the underlying business units and teams, and finally linking the team scorecard to the individual performance plan of the employees. This top-down and bottom-up process is implemented, step by step, by all successive organization levels in increasing detail (see Chapter 7). In this way, the overall strategy of the organization (OBSC) is systematically translated into more specific plans on each organization level.

Personal Balanced Scorecard, pages 153–161

This is needed to shift the strategic vision into action. Every individual on all these organizational levels formulates his/her own PBSC and shares this with colleagues.

3. **Improving**—This means continuously improving yourself and your work. It concerns the implementation of personal and organizational improvement actions based on the PBSC and the OBSC respectively. The focus here is on correcting mistakes, improving existing capabilities, doing things right the first time, and acquiring new skills and capabilities through gradual improvement. The personal improvement actions are implemented according to the Plan-Do-Act-Challenge cycle (see Chapter 3). This results in a steady increase in happiness, awareness, enjoyment, pleasure, learning and creativity; at work as well as in free time. Table 9.1 shows a summary of the activities that you should consider in this process of personal improvement. The alignment of personal ambition with personal behavior is also part of this process (see Chapter 4). I recommend reading *The Top 200 Secrets of Success and the Pillars of Self-Mastery* by Robin Sharma. It contains a wealth of wisdom and powerful insights for further developing your character and tackling your weaknesses. Organizational improvement actions are implemented according to Deming's Plan-Do-Check-Act cycle. This cycle consists of the following four phases: 1) *Plan* (develop an improvement plan); 2) *Do* (execute this improvement plan on a limited scale); 3) *Check* (review the results of the improvement actions; and 4) *Act* (implement the proven improvements). Table 9.2 shows a summary of activities you should consider in the organizational improvement process, which are linked to Total Quality Management (Rampersad, 2005).
4. **Developing and learning**—Here, the emphasis is on job-related talent management and learning. To be able to manage and use the talents within the organization effectively, it is necessary to embed the personal and organizational balanced scorecards in the ambition meeting and in the talent management process (see Chapter 8). This is done on the basis of the talent management cycle introduced in this book, which consists of the following phases—Result Planning, Coaching, Appraisal and Talent Development. The learning process in this phase encompasses the review of the scorecards, the actualization of these scorecards based on changing conditions, the documentation of the lessons learned, and checking which things went well and which went wrong during the previous phases. Depending on these evaluation results, the implementation or the formulation of the scorecards may be adjusted. This phase deals with learning from gained experiences. It refers to internalizing acquired knowledge and actualizing it through experience in order to change

both the individual and collective behavior of employees, thus enabling the organization to perform better. The concordance of personal ambition and the shared organizational ambition takes place at all levels of the organization (see Chapter 5). The alignment of the shared ambition with business ethics also takes place in this phase of the PBSC cycle (see Chapter 6).

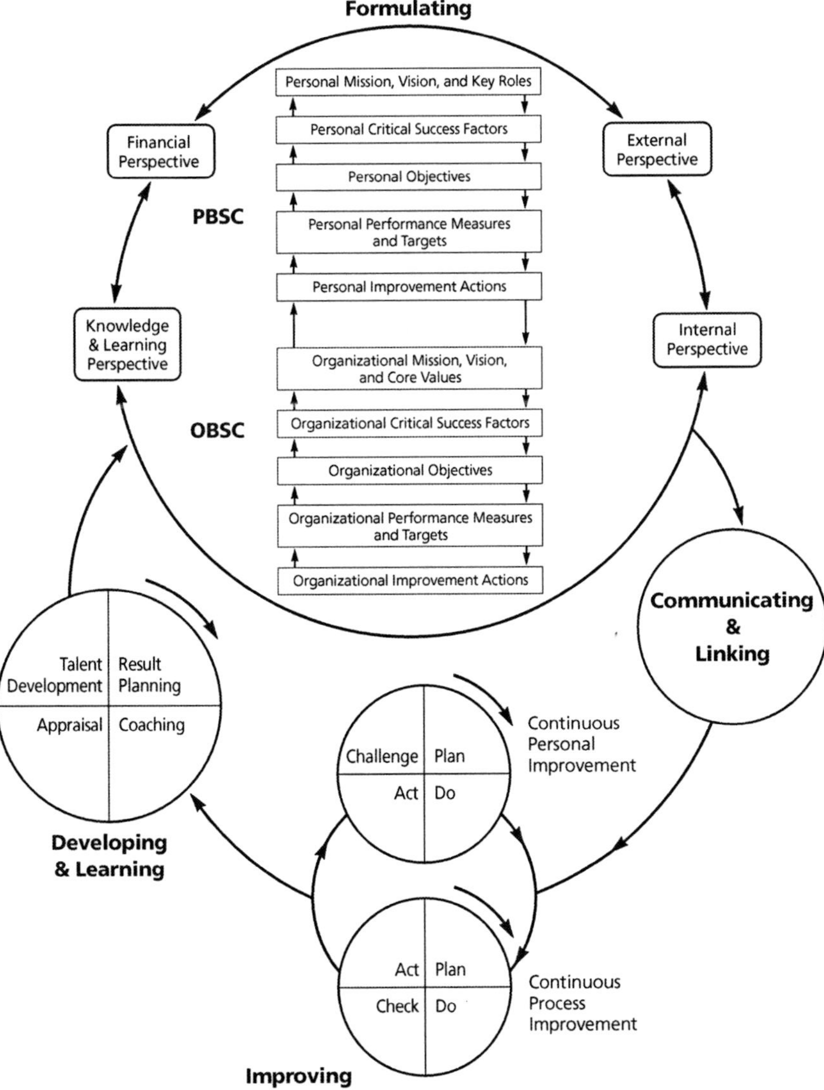

Figure 9.1. The PBSC Cycle (© Hubert Rampersad)

Table 9.1. Summary of Personal Improvement Activities (Related to the PBSC and the Plan–Do–Act–Challenge cycle)

- Understand yourself.
- Recognize your responsibility and ethical duty to make personal improvement a routine and a continuous process.
- Assess relationships with your family, supervisor, peers, subordinates, customers, and others.
- Regularly evaluate your need/desire to improve and the necessity of personal growth.
- Formulate and examine your PBSC and apply this to your non-work life as well.
- Share this with a trusted person (family, supervisor, colleague, subordinate, and/or customer).
- Obtain your supervisor's agreement on the job-related PBSC elements before proceeding.
- Start off with the implementation of your PBSC according to the Plan–Do–Act–Challenge cycle.
- Improve and monitor your actions and thoughts continuously based on your PBSC.
- Ask for the trusted person's comments and perceptions.
- Also focus on the things that you are not good at, habits that limit you, and habits that have an unfavorable influence on your life and deliver poor results.
- Review the results according to the personal performance measures and targets earlier defined.
- Check to what extent you have realized your personal objectives and adjust your PBSC if needed.
- Achieve behavioral changes and constantly challenge your behavior.
- Make time in your schedule to improve and to help others improve.
- Attend to your continued education and see your job as a learning experience.
- Take advantage of learning opportunities and take initiative.
- Understand the capabilities and limitations of your processes, and your customers' needs and expectations.
- Pursue innovation and new ideas based on Plan-Do-Act-Challenge cycle.
- Be observant, a good listener, and remove the barriers you normally erect.
- Maintain a positive attitude toward life and never get carried away by anger.
- Perform the breathing and silence exercise regularly; for 20 minutes in the morning and in the evening.
- Demonstrate commitment and leadership, set an example.
- Foster co-operation and communication.
- Avoid extreme behavior and remain calm.
- Trust others and be worthy of their trust.
- Find a balance between your personal ambition and your behavior.
- Have respect for others and speak honestly and well of others.
- Be the most honest person that you know; be trustworthy.
- Judge others fairly and correctly.

Table 9.1. Summary of Personal Improvement Activities (Related to the PBSC and the Plan–Do–Act–Challenge cycle) (Cont.)

- Communicate effectively; the quality of your life is the quality of your communication with others and yourself.
- Cultivate and foster new friendships, especially with those who have shared many experiences and laughs with you; relationships are essential for maintaining a healthy and successful life.
- Show compassion and sincere consideration for all your friends and develop long-lasting friendships by being a good friend.
- Treat everyone who crosses your path as if he/she is the most important person in your world.
- Overlook the weaknesses of others and see the good that each inherently possesses. We can learn from everyone. Be open to this.
- Develop the habit of punctuality; it reflects discipline and a proper regard for others.
- Revive your habit of laughter.
- Learn to be still and enjoy the power of silence for at least ten minutes a day.
- Speak less; listen 60% of the time. You will learn much, as everyone we meet, every day has something to teach us. Listening is the beginning of all wisdom. Learning is listening effectively.
- Learn to always think positively; when a negative thought comes to your mind, immediately replace it with one that is positive.
- Dedicate yourself to leaving a powerful legacy to the world.
- Be truthful, patient, persevering, modest and generous; be someone with a warm heart and great character.
- See every opportunity as a chance to learn.
- Be an explorer; find pleasure in the things that others take for granted.
- Develop your ability to focus for extended periods of time and to build your concentration.
- Have courage and inspire others with your actions.
- Take anyone you think is highly effective and ethical as your role model. Visualize this person and do like him/her.
- Never feel that you have no time for new ideas, you are investing in yourself.
- Become an adventurer and revitalize your spirit and sense of playfulness. Take time out for the renewal of your mind, body and spirit.
- Follow your conscience.
- Never do anything you wouldn't be proud to tell your mother.
- Know your best qualities and cultivate them.
- Never complain, be known as a positive, strong, energetic and enthusiastic person.
- Fill your mind with thoughts of serenity, positivity, strength, courage and compassion.
- Create an image of yourself as a highly competent, strong, disciplined, calm and decent individual.
- Schedule relaxation time into your week; spend time in reflection, unwinding and recharging your batteries.

Table 9.1. Summary of Personal Improvement Activities (Related to the PBSC and the Plan–Do–Act–Challenge cycle) (Cont.)

- Make time for the things that matter most; choose what is important and filter out what is of no value. Focus on those objectives that are truly important; read only those materials that will be useful to you.
- Be disciplined in following the schedule of your PBSC.
- Seek out knowledge. Knowledge is power. The more you know, the less you fear. The more one knows, the more one achieves.
- Read more, learn more, laugh more and love more.
- Show your appreciation and respect for your loved ones.
- The essence of a person is his character; make yours unique, unblemished and strong.
- Place greater importance on staying happy than amassing material possessions; be happy with what you have.
- Strive to be humble and live a simple, uncluttered and productive existence.
- Be committed to what you are doing and to being a better parent, friend and citizen.
- Be known as an idea person, willing to take on challenges and tackle them with passion and enthusiasm.
- Spend at least half an hour every day alone—in peaceful introspection, reading or just relaxing.
- Cultivate the habit of optimism.
- Develop a focused state of mind. Pay attention to your spiritual development so as to gain greater self-confidence.
- Give attention to the development of spirit, health, and useful activities; you cannot do good unless you feel good. When you are serene, relaxed and enthusiastic you are also more productive, creative and dynamic.
- Dedicate yourself to higher knowledge and to the development of a higher level of consciousness.
- Always pursue your personal objectives.
- Be in control of yourself and live in harmony with your personal mission, vision, and key roles.
- Align your personal ambition with your personal behavior and match it with the organizational ambition.
- Assess the results and evaluate your improvement.
- Learn to measure and understand processes and to use data that support your decisions.
- Recognize the processes you use and understand how they are linked to others.
- Know your internal and external customers. You should know and understand your colleagues and clients, not only yourself.
- Document the lessons learned.
- Celebrate your success.
- Successively select a more difficult personal objective with the corresponding improvement action from your PBSC, and start working on it.

Table 9.2. Summary of Organizational Improvement Activities (related to the OBSC and the Plan-Do-Check-Act cycle)

Process Selection and Definition	*Process Evaluation and Standardization*	*Process Improvement*
Set the stage for process improvement	**Process evaluation**	• Analyze available process data
• Apply the TPS Life Cycle Scan	• Describe the selected business process in detail	• Update the improvement plan
• Recognize the need to change and discuss this throughout the organization	• Measure and review process performances	• Determine improvement objectives
• Establish a vision for the organization	• Identifying process shortcomings	• Indicate improvement actions
• Formulate the Organizational Balanced Scorecard (OBSC)	• Analyze process problems	• Identify process measures
• Deploy the OBSC into the organization	• Analyze available process data	• Plan data collection strategy
• Make a long-term commitment	• Perform cause-and-effect analyses	• Train to the improvement plan
• Demonstrate top-management commitment	• Identify root causes	• Enable the plan
• Remove obvious barriers to improvement	• Assess process stability	• Conduct cause-and-effect analyses
• Eliminate sources of fear using the TPS and PBSC concept	• Analyze special causes of variation	• Develop solutions
• Establish a personnel and customer focus	• Correct special causes	• Test the selected solutions
• Understand employee and customer needs and expectations	• Bring the business process under control	• Conduct experiments with process changes
• Encourage individual effort	**Process standardization**	• Observe and analyze the data
• Stimulate creative thinking according to the PBSC and the Plan–Do–Act–Challenge cycle	• Standardize process execution	• Look for patterns in the data
• Inform and involve everyone, including customers and suppliers	• Communicate and promote standards	• Compare the data with the theory
• Define learning needs	• Train employees in the use of the standards	• Measure the effects and review the results
• Make training and education a high priority	• Enable and enforce the standards	• Determine whether the objectives are met
	• Measure results against standards	• Respond to deviation from the plan
	• Respond to deviations from standards	• Identify root causes
	• Identify root causes of variation	• Correct special causes immediately
	• Analyze common causes of variation	• Look for alternative solutions
	• Reduce variation in process	• Implement the desired improvement

Table 9.2. Summary of Organizational Improvement Activities (related to the OBSC and the Plan-Do-Check-Act cycle) (Cont.)

Process Selection and Definition	*Process Evaluation and Standardization*	*Process Improvement*
• Recognize and reward learning achievement • Cultivate leadership • Form a steering group **Select a business process to improve** • Define critical processes related to the OBSC • Identify opportunities • Set priorities and select the most important critical business process • Appoint a process owner • Install an improvement team • Train the team in the use of improvement methods and techniques • Discuss the organizational vision and business strategy in the team **Define the business process** • Describe and flow chart the business process • Identify supplier/customer relationship • Identify key measures to meet customer needs and expectations • Ensure capable measurement system • Formulate an improvement plan • Gather necessary information	• Prevent recurring deviation from standards • Streamline the process • Error-proof the process • Institute total productive maintenance and total performance scorecard • Document lessons learned • Collect and maintain process performance data	• Bring the process under control • Implement permanent change in the process • Asses the results • Continue to collect and analyze data • Continuously monitor the process • Prevent recurring deviation • Redesign products or business processes • Document improved performance • Standardize changes • Document the improved process • Document project results • Make final presentation • Evaluate team methods • Evaluate project results • Recommend follow-up activities • Celebrate the process improvement cycle completion • Recognize and reward continuous improvement behavior • Repeat the PDCA cycle • Select a new business process to improve

As we can see from Figure 9.1, the PBSC cycle consists of a number of large and small wheels. These all need to be interrelated and to turn in the right direction in order to get the larger PBSC wheel moving successfully. The model gives us insight into both the way this wheel can be mobilized and the coherence between its different aspects. After the last phase is complete, the cycle is again followed in order to align the scorecards with its surroundings on a continuous basis. Thus your organization will come to know itself and its surroundings and so improve itself. Naturally, the same applies to you, i.e. by reviewing your PBSC monthly with a trusted person and learning from your previous experiences, you will know both yourself and your surroundings better, which will allow you to improve yourself. By doing this you will constantly improve your performance, and thus continuously satisfy yourself and others. Strategy formation, improvement, development of human potential, and learning are all part of a perpetual process.

Progressing through the PBSC cycle will result in the continuous improvement of business results through the years. Through this approach the customer is satisfied, and the organization is able to come to know itself and its surroundings on an ongoing basis. TPS Soft (see Appendix I) is a knowledge-based and interactive software system that will assist you with the implementation of the PBSC system in order to realize this objective. It offers management and HR the possibility to effectively steer their organization to better performance, happiness, and motivation. The TPS Life Cycle Scan (see Appendix II) is a performance excellence model that will guide you in this process of total performance improvement. It's a measuring rod that is laid against the organization to define which development phase it is in, and the total score it has obtained.

EPILOGUE

Doing good to others is not a duty. It's a joy for it. It increases your own wealth and happiness.

—Zoroaster

I have written this book because I want to help make people happier and more active, creative and ethical, at work as well as away from work. By way of this book, I want to provide them some new tools, tested in practice, so that they can master themselves, gain more understanding for self-responsibility, create a stable basis for their growth, let them create their own future and discover their destiny. I want them to understand that personal development is a person's own responsibility. It is their ethical duty and responsibility to develop their self and become more proactive, for their own good, their loved ones, their work, their organization, their country, and the world they are part of. I want them to understand that freedom and inner peace comes from within and that this can be realized in a simple manner.

Also, I want managers to understand that they can improve the quality of life of their customers and make them happy, if they improve the quality of life of their co-workers and make them happy first. I want human resources staff to understand that a healthy family situation of the co-workers has an important impact on their functioning at work and they should not ignore this fact. They can encourage their employees to systematically use their Personal Balanced Scorecard within their family and to help improve the co-workers' home situation on the basis of the PDAC cycle. Through this book I also want to reduce the gap between company life and life outside the company, and between the way people deal with their colleagues at work and the way they act with their friends and family outside their jobs. What I also have in mind with this book is

Personal Balanced Scorecard, pages 163–165

to drive out fear from organizations and to create a way of life within organizations, which is characterized by freedom, trust, enjoyment, motivation, self-awareness, ethical behavior and learning, so that individuals and organizations can deliver sustainable top performance and enhance their value. My aim with PBSC is to make companies more "human." This is one of the most important challenges in the corporate world and one that we must focus on. I consider it indeed my ethical duty to do something useful for society, of which we are all a part. The foundation is in my own personal mission: "*Sharing knowledge is joy, especially if, by doing this, my work can mean something in the life of others.*" Read this book over and over and share it with others.

I believe this book differs in a number of essential points from most other management books in the field. It is up to you, the reader, to judge whether this is true. I gladly welcome any reactions and suggestions from you regarding this book. Please send your feedback by e-mail to h.rampersad@tps-international.com. The development of the Personal Balanced Scorecard concept and the writing of this book has been a continuous learning process. If you want to keep track of the new developments in this field, visit the website: *www.Total-Performance-Scorecard.com*. Total Performance Scorecard™ and Personal Balanced Scorecard™ are worldwide registered trade marks. We are devoted to helping individuals and organizations become more successful. We provide integrated and sustainable professional services (consulting and training) based on the proven Total Performance Scorecard and Personal Balanced Scorecard principles. The results are individual and organizational effectiveness and a related unique competitive advantage. For more information about the Total Performance Scorecard and Personal Balanced Scorecard concept, or the international office closest to you, please write to the addresses mentioned overleaf.

United States

TPS International Inc.
P.O. Box 3361; Costa Mesa, CA 92628
Phone: 323-491-7424
h.rampersad@tps-international.com
info@total-performance-scorecard.com
www.total-performance-scorecard.com

Total Performance Scorecard™
TPS

TPS Great Lakes Inc.
1492 E. Drahner Road
Michigan, US 48371, USA
Phone: 416-961-2487
Fax: 416-929-2018
e.lester@tps-international.com
r.bowden@tps-international.com
www.total-performance-scorecard.com

Personal Balanced Scorecard™
PBSC

Canada

TPS Performance Canada Ltd.
1 Balmoral Avenue, Suite 617
Toronto, Ontario
Canada M4V 3B9
Phone: (416) 972-9196
Fax:(416) 972-9261
b.angel@tps-international.com
www.total-performance-scorecard.com

Netherlands

TPS Consulting Netherlands
Riet Blom-Mouritsstraat 27
3066 GL Rotterdam
Netherlands
Tel: +31-653831159
info@total-performance-scorecard.com
www.Total-Performance-Scorecard.com

Germany

TPS Germany GmbH
Köningsallee 60 F, 40212 Düsseldorf, Germany
Tel.: +49 211 8903 681, Fax: +49 211 8903 999
tps-germany@total-performance-scorecard.com
www.total-performance-scorecard.com

South America

TPS–PERFORMANCE DO BRASIL
Av. Brig. Faria Lima 1931, 10 andar
01451-917 - São Paulo - SP - Brasil
Tel: +55-11-3816-3144
Fax: +55-11-3819-9621
jorge@ml.com.br
www.tpsbrasil.com.br

Asia-Pacific

PT. TPS Consulting Indonesia
J.l. Melawai XII-XIII Blok N-1
Kebayoran Baru, Jakarta 12160, Indonesia
Phone: +62-21-7278-7276
Fax: +62-21-7278-7276
indra.uno@tps-indonesia.com
www.tps-indonesia.com

APPENDIX I

TPS SOFT

TPS Soft is an interactive software system that will assist you with the implementation of the Personal Balanced Scorecard and the Total Performance Scorecard. It offers management and HR the possibility to effectively steer their organization on performance, happiness, joy and motivation. This software system consists of the following parts:

1. Personal Balanced Scorecard (PBSC)
2. Organizational Balanced Scorecard (OBSC)
3. Match between the PBSC and the OBSC
4. Effectively managing of talent within the organization.

Every employee owns responsibility for the filling-in of his/her own PBSC. The first step is the creation of an employee's profile. This offers the possibility to benchmark one employee against others as explained below. Subsequently the employee formulates from every perspective, his/her personal ambition and the related objectives, performance indicators, targets and improvement actions. Possibilities are available to make use of a predefined set of data or numerous examples in the system. Doing this, and using these possibilities, the employee will obtain an improved understanding of him/her self and have the opportunity to manage and coach him/her self in a goal-oriented way. The status of his/her improvement actions is made visible through unambiguous indicators at any given moment. After being authorized by the employee, others can provide feedback on his/her actions at any moment. Targets that have been achieved

Personal Balanced Scorecard, pages 167–168

and challenges that have been taken up can also be brought up-to-date immediately. The TPS Code of Ethics is being applied here; this implies that the system respects the individual employee's privacy and that no personal information can be shared with unauthorized others. Another benefit of the system is that any employee can benchmark him/her self against any other employee with the same profile, from inside and from outside the own organization. The TPS database also contains demographic data so that the possibility exists to compare with other like-minded individuals. The PBSC is connected to a knowledge database that gives feedback and advice to further improve oneself. The match between personal and organizational ambition is also achieved by comparing the personal targets and objectives of the employee with the organizational targets and objectives as formulated in the OBSC. Other contributions to this match are given through the filling-in of interactive questionnaires and the recording of results of the ambition meetings. The result is a clear overview of the similarities and differences between the PBSC of the employee and the OBSC of the organization. These results contain valuable information for the HR manager to be able to effectively manage the talents that exist within the organization. Please visit www.total-performance-scorecard.com for further details and the latest information about TPS Soft.

For further information regarding TPS Soft

TPS International Inc.
P.O. Box 3361; Costa Mesa, CA 92628
Phone: 323-491-7424
h.rampersad@tps-international.com
info@total-performance-scorecard.com
www.total-performance-scorecard.com

APPENDIX II

TPS LIFE CYCLE SCAN

An organization's performance readiness and requirements for improvement are dependent on its stage of performance development. An assessment of the organization's current development level will point to (1) the organization's current state of performance culture development, (2) its readiness for the Total Performance Scorecard Plan-Do-Act-Challenge performance improvement methodology, and (3) a plan to transition the organization to a higher culture and performance level. Most organizations span more than one level, so a complex set of PBSC and TPS requirements should be expected to be indicated. It is possible but rare that an organization can successfully jump several levels, at least in all dimensions, so progressive improvement might be called for. This fits with the highly strategic nature of the PBSC and TPS implementation—addressing organization-employee strategy and goal alignment in order to bring about a strategic and sustainable shift upwards in performance culture.

The TPS Life Cycle Scan is a performance excellence model aimed at personal and organizational performance improvement. It is a holistic instrument for systematic self-diagnosis that will help both public and private sector organizations to increase individual and organizational performance in the direction of total performance. We present five development levels and eight dimensions that follow TPS and PBSC concepts. These levels and dimensions indicate the organization's level of performance maturity compared with that needed to excel in management. The five development levels are: *basic, improving, moderate, advanced, and total performance*. Each higher

Personal Balanced Scorecard, pages 169–180

level, i.e., towards total performance, can be considered as an increase in the organization's abilities to adapt and react to external and internal necessity for improved performance. The TPS Life Cycle Scan is a measuring rod that can augment existing approaches being used by the organization. It helps to define in which development level overall and for specific topics it finds itself by its total TPS Life Cycle Scan score. By making performance management measurable in this way, it will be easier to manage related performance processes and to increase the score year by year. This makes it possible to steer improvement actions systematically, always aiming for higher levels of personal and business excellence.

Five Levels of Development in TPS

Level 1) Basic performance: Hardly any attention is given to personal and organizational performance measurement, process mindedness, personal integrity, and knowledge and talent management. Management is hierarchical. Performance measurement is confined to the organization's financial statements, deciding on pay raises for employees, and transactional process improvements. No attention is given to the performance implications of personal integrity. As a consequence, there is mutual distrust and loss of talent in the organization.

Level 2) Improving performance: Sporadic and ad hoc manual attention is given to measuring personal and organizational performance. Some organizational data is extracted from the organization's systems for reporting and budgeting support. Any process mind set is only related to risk reduction, while performance implications of personal integrity are only related to regulatory compliance. Management is still hierarchical but has instituted a variable compensation program. Performance improvement depends on quarter-to-quarter extraordinary ad hoc actions, and tends to fall short of expectations.

Level 3) Moderate performance: Measurement of personal and organizational performance is selective. An organizational balanced scorecard is produced. Personal integrity and the management of knowledge and talent improvements result from implementing regulatory compliance recommendations. ISO 9000 may be present in the organization. The performance of the organization is starting to improve selectively beyond previous expectations.

Level 4) Advanced performance: Measurement of personal and organizational performance is structured and systematic. TQM has been implemented on a strategic level as well as on a tactical level. Ambition meetings and talent management are implemented at the executive level. Process improvement is driven by qualitative and quantitative metrics. Personal integrity is starting to be managed in a systematic and structured way. At this stage, some departments are piloting important

TPS elements at the strategic level, including the PBSC, OBSC, ambition meetings, talent management. Parts of the organization may qualify for TPS Distinction.

Level 5) Total performance: TPS has become a natural and continuous learning process that runs smoothly and spontaneously. Personal and organizational performance measurement, a customer-oriented process mind set, personal integrity, and the systematic management of knowledge and talent all have highest priority. All key elements of TPS have been implemented throughout the organization on strategic, tactical, operational, and individual levels. There is a learning culture in which self-learning, self-consciousness, awareness and acceptance of individual responsibility, enjoyment, pro-active ethical behavior, and a focus on performance are a "way of life", both at work and in life. Because the many challenges are matched by related new skills or capabilities, people are motivated and fulfilled, enjoy their work, and use their non-work time more effectively. The performance of this organization is classified as *total* on the basis of these characteristics. The entire organization qualifies for the TPS certification on the basis of this result, and is considered to be *Best Practice.*

Normally, we expect to see organizations that have not adopted the principles outlined in this book being in Levels 1, 2 or 3. The organizations that have are now typically in Level 4 and moving on to Level 5.

Table AII.1 Eight TPS Dimensions

1. Personal management	*The way individuals are encouraged to increase their self-knowledge, awareness and consciousness and to increase their personal and professional effectiveness. This allows them to participate fully and authentically at work and home, reducing stress and ensuring a creative, productive work environment, which captures and values the intelligence of each employee.*
1.1 Personal ambition	I gain self-knowledge and develop my self-awareness and personal responsibility continuously, by formulating my personal ambition (personal vision and mission and key roles) authentically; I continually strive to reach higher levels of accomplishment and mindset change. My personal ambition is a living concept that I hone throughout my life.
1.2 Personal strategy roadmapping and life-career planning	I have formulated my personal balanced scorecard (PBSC); I make career and personal lifestyle choices, I set goals for continuous improvement, track my accomplishments and use the PBSC as an external reminder of my internal priorities.

Table AII.1 Eight TPS Dimensions (Cont.)

1.3 Personal improvement	I recognize my responsibilities to continuously improve myself, based on my PBSC and the Plan–Do–Act–Challenge cycle. So I constantly become more conscious, authentic, creative and thus, increase my personal effectiveness.
1.4 Personal work/life balance	I consciously and continuously seek to balance my work and personal life guided by my personal balanced scorecard and the Plan-Do-Act-Challenge cycle, and I use my time more effectively,
1.5 Personal leadership	I see myself as a leader, continuously achieve results and effectively manage the internal and external principles on which these results are based, using a leadership style founded on authenticity, intuition, dependability, openness, integrity, and trust.
1.6 Serving leadership	As a leader, I continuously put myself at the service of my colleagues and employees in a trustful manner; I spontaneously inspire, stimulate, help, and encourage them, listen to them, and appreciate their contributions.
2. Strategic management	*The way the organization's vision, mission and core values (shared ambition) are formulated by the stakeholders and translated into concrete organizational objectives, targets, performance indicators, and improvement actions aimed at achieving and sustaining competitive advantage.*
2.1 Shared ambition	The organization has a collective mission, vision and core values reflecting the aspirations of the stakeholders. I identify with the shared ambition and it provides guidance and focus for me.
2.2 Business strategy roadmapping	The organization has formulated an organizational balanced scorecard (OBSC) effectively with shared ambition translated strategically into organizational critical success factors, objectives, performance measures, targets, and creative strategies. Progress is tracked and the OBSC is constantly used as a reminder of organizational priorities.
2.3 Customer-centric strategies	The needs of internal and external customers are reflected in the creative strategies set out in the OBSC. We consciously take actions based on this to improve customer satisfaction, relationships, and predict future needs.
2.4 Organizational improvement	The corporate balanced scorecard is implemented across the organization, to measure business performance against key metrics. Organizational improvement is a continuous process based on the OBSC and according to the Plan–Do–Check–Act cycle, in order to achieve desired results.
2.5 Strategy communication	The corporate balanced scorecard is communicated timely, honestly, clearly, frequently and face-to-face with all stakeholders to renew ownership and commitment at all organizational levels. Is two-way communication encouraged?

Table AII.1 Eight TPS Dimensions (Cont.)

2.6 Scorecard deployment	The organizational balanced scorecard is systematically cascaded through the organization using departmental scorecards (tactical level), team scorecards (operational level), and individual performance plans (individual level).
3. Business values management	*The way the organization concretely interprets and behaves according to high ethical norms, values and principles.*
3.1 Personal integrity	I take personal responsibility to act in accordance with my conscience, creating a continuous balance between my personal ambition and my behavior. I strive to live authentically and it is a continuous learning process.
3.2 Business integrity	This organization acts ethically towards all stakeholders; Ethical awareness and behavior is valued and encouraged and is integrated into our policies, practices and decision-making. It is integral to our culture.
3.3 Social responsibility	The organization defines and implements fair, respectful and considerate treatment of its employees at all levels and in all roles; we continuously consider the economic, social and environmental impacts of our activities and have formal structures in place to sustain the effort.
3.4 Transparency and accountability	The organization acts routinely according to its code of conduct and ethics which is lived by all employees, and is obvious to all stakeholders. We regularly publish detailed reports on our own citizenship and business activities, including specific ethics initiatives. Fairness and consistency in behavior and compensation is indisputable.
3.5 Regulatory compliance	Our organization spontaneously complies with all local, state and federal regulations including corporate governance in spirit as well as in word
3.6 Branding and trust	We take pride in having a brand name that is synonymous with trust in the eyes of our stakeholders. Our integrity is recognized by our competitors and other non-stakeholders.
4. Talent management	*The way talents in the organization are being effectively managed, succession is planned and developed across the enterprise, maximum self development of the employees is realized, talents are optimally deployed, and the employees rewarded. and recognized.*
4.1 Individual competencies	My manager and I develop and review a manageable set of job-oriented competencies needed for my talent development and growth aimed at optimizing the outcome of the shared ambition; This is my individual performance plan.
4.2 Individual capability and performance planning	My manager and I initiate periodic discussions (agreements) to optimize my performance and improve my competencies guided by my individual performance plan. Some job-related elements of my PBSC are included in these agreements. There is also a periodical, informal, voluntary and confidential ambition meeting between my

Table AII.1 Eight TPS Dimensions (Cont.)

	manager and me with my PBSC as the topic and in which my manager acts as a trusted informal coach.
4.3 Review & mentoring	I am effectively being guided by my manager to help me optimize my performance. My manager coaches me at fixed intervals on my progress. During this meeting, I receive individual guidance and feedback, we agree on deliverables, and define new skills which are to be developed to fit my competencies.
4.4 Talent development	Training of employees is a high priority. Employees constantly receive training to obtain new insights and acquire new skills by their direct managers using "learning by doing" and "on the job" principles to enable them to work smarter and fulfill their role effectively.
4.5 Job-related career planning	I have a career counseling session with my manager once a year based on my PBSC and individual performance plan. This provides me new development directions to take on new roles inside and outside the organization.
4.6 Succession planning	There are highly qualified people in all positions within our organization. We are recruiting employees based on the PBSC system to ensure the necessary job fit by matching the personal ambition with the requirements of the job and with the shared ambition.
5. Process management	*The way business processes are constantly being evaluated and modified or reframed and reformulated to continuously improve the satisfaction of Internal and external customers.*
5.1 Customer definition	External and internal customers are both defined according to the principles of TQM. These are continuously and routinely being satisfied.
5.2 Customer needs	Customer needs are continuously and systematically surveyed, understood and fed back into product and process improvements as well the development of new products and services.
5.3 Customer value & process definition	The organization has defined which business processes are adding value to the customer and related key metrics of process measurement and improvement
5.4 Process evaluation & standardization	All business processes are described, understood and standardized in order to continuously fulfill the customer's desires. The standard procedures are being used routinely and spontaneously.
5.5 Process & performance measurement	The effectiveness of all our business processes is being measured and monitored continuously based on performance measures.
5.6 Continuous process improvement	All business processes are continuously, spontaneously and pro-actively improved in a 'project approach' according to the Plan-Do-Check-Act cycle and using lean techniques, reflecting both internal and external customer needs.

Table AII.1 Eight TPS Dimensions (Cont.)

6. Knowledge management	*The way the organization's learning is increased and the knowledge stream managed; the way we develop, transfer, use and mobilize knowledge to create a climate for sustainable innovation.*
6.1 Self-knowledge	I continuously develop self-knowledge based on my PBSC and according to the Plan-Do-Act-Challenge cycle, to increase my creativity.
6.2 Self-learning	I am learning spontaneously and experience a continuous personal transformation based on my PBSC and according to the Plan-Do-Act-Challenge cycle. I get enough room and complete freedom to take on challenges, to learn, to take action, to make informal contacts, to gain experience, to take initiatives, to experiment and to take risks. There is a safe environment to constantly practice, try new things and to make mistakes.
6.3 Shared knowledge	Knowledge within our organization is managed in such a way that we spontaneously and intensively share knowledge with each other. The knowledge flow is being managed effectively. The continuous and intensive generation, cultivation, updating, mobilization, application and sharing of relevant knowledge is a way of life in the organization.
6.4 Shared learning	We are learning together and from each other spontaneously and intensively. The culture supports this process in all divisions and based on this we are encouraged to continually improve.
6.5 Problem solving	Collaborative and individual problem-solving is a pro-active part of each person's daily work based on TQM principles. We solve common problems routinely and systematically in multidisciplinary teams and creativity is valued.
6.6 Knowledge infrastructure	We have an effective knowledge infrastructure of tools, systems, continuous training, brainstorm sessions, and review meetings that supports which facilitates all facets of the organizational learning process and which continuously stimulates creativity, systems thinking, self-confidence, innovations, and a conducive learning environment.
7. Team management	*The way individuals within the organization feel committed to shared ambition, and accept, acknowledge, trust, respect, and need each other—in order to achieve results together—characterized by individuals within the company sharing knowledge, work, thoughts, feelings, excitement, satisfaction, pressure, pleasure, emotions, doubts, and successes with each other.*
7.1 Team balance	There is combined action between complementary competencies and personalities and a balance of learning styles within and across all teams. The formulated personal ambition of potential team members is being used as a guideline when putting together teams.

Table AII.1 Eight TPS Dimensions (Cont.)

7.2 Team development	There is harmonious collaboration in my team led by team spirit, strong connection between all team members. Team members know, trust, respect, understand and complete each other.
7.3 Team learning	We share our PBSCs with each other spontaneously. As a result there's team learning based on trust and respect. Our personal ambitions are in line with the ambition of our team.
7.4 Team diversity	Team members unconditionally acknowledge and accept each other's diversity differences. There's respect and mutual understanding in my team.
7.5 Team measurement and performance	The effectiveness of my team is constantly being measured and evaluated, in order to achieve high team performance. The team results are a combined effort of all team members. All team members feel responsible for the team results and are constantly being informed about the team results.
7.6 Team communication	The team ensures adequate communication on the team's mission and progress to stakeholders external to the team
8. Change management	*The way organization support for change is created and change is managed effectively.*
8.1 Change infrastructure	Changes are integrally and systematically being dealt with in a structured way based on a steering group, project group, TPS-manager, sponsorship and improvement teams.
8.2 Cultural environment	The organization culture is characterized by openness towards newcomers and outsiders, dedication, willingness to learn, and inner involvement. The organization is open to and embraces change and has an attitude inclusion and mutual trust.
8.3 Customer culture	Our total organization is customer minded, the market guides us. We recognize and accommodate the customer culture.
8.4 Managing change resistance	Resistance to change is recognized and mitigated in the organization. We totally stand behind change and are convinced it leads to improvement. It is regarded as a challenge.
8.5 Implementing change	Our executives and managers are committed to supporting change, which is demonstrated across the entire organization. All stakeholders are constantly being included when making decisions about change. The what, why, how and the consequences of change are constantly, honestly, timely, consistently, decisively and face-to-face being communicated to employees by the top management. Change proposals are underpinned with clear arguments.
8.6 Change sustainability	Employees first take the responsibility to change themselves according to their PBSC and the PDAC-cycle. This forms a starting point to durable cultural change.

HOW IS THE TPS SELF-ASSESSMENT EXECUTED?

The TPS self-assessment system is a matrix in which the five development phases are indicated horizontally and the dimensions and sub-dimensions vertically. The sub-dimensions are derived from the TPS concept, with each sub-dimension having its own weighting factor. The matrix is graded from right to left; moving to the right side of the matrix means the higher one appraises the organization. At the intersection of a development phase and a dimension, statements are given that are characteristic for the organization in that specific phase. Table AII.2 shows the dimension Personal Management from the matrix. The individual indicates a view of the organization's position in each sub-dimension by selecting the statement that corresponds most with the perceived situation in the organization. Our related software system subsequently calculates the total score of each of the development phases for each dimension. The completed lists will then be processed automatically and visualized in a spider diagram format. This spider diagram is a graphic presentation of the position of the organization in the eight dimensions and the five development phases. You quickly and easily obtain an insight into which dimensions the organization scores highly in and which dimensions deserve special attention. By making performance management measurable in this way, it is easier to manage the related processes and to seek to increase your the score year by year. The TPS Life Cycle Scan will guide organizations in a systematic manner in their striving for personal and business excellence in accordance with the Total Performance Scorecard.

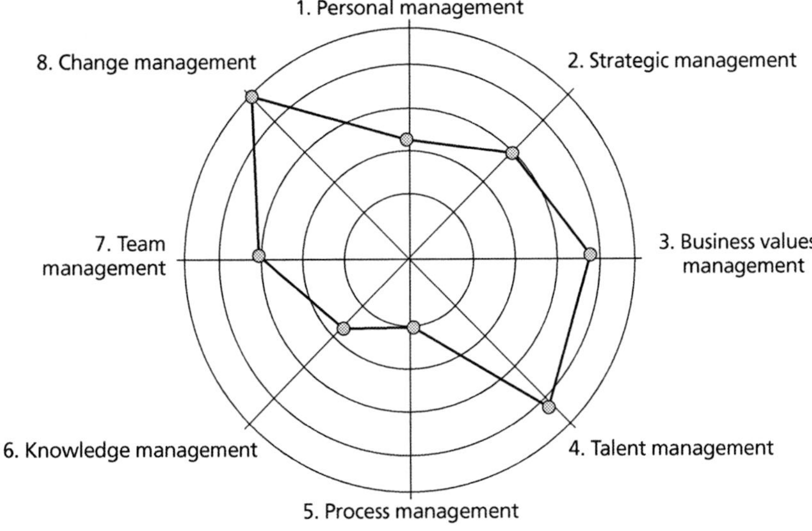

Spider diagram

Table AII.2 The Dimension Personal Management

1. Personal management	*Basic performance*	*Improving performance*	*Moderate performance*	*Advanced performance*	*Total performance*
1.1 Personal ambition	❑ I do not have any mechanism to gain insight into myself, to reach higher levels of accomplishment.	❑ I reflect on my motivations and consequent actions on an ad hoc basis to reach higher levels of accomplishment.	❑ I regularly reflect on my motivations and consequent actions to reach higher levels of accomplishment	❑ I gain self-knowledge based on my formulated personal ambition. I continuously reflect on this to reach higher levels of accomplishment and mindset change.	❑ I gain self-knowledge and develop my self-awareness and personal responsibility continuously, by formulating my personal ambition (personal vision, mission and key roles) authentically; I continually strive to reach higher levels of accomplishment and mindset change. My personal ambition is a living concept that I hone throughout my life.
1.2 Personal strategy roadmapping and life-career planning	❑ I do not have a mechanism to formulate personal career and lifestyle objectives.	❑ I have informally formulated some personal career and lifestyle objectives.	❑ I have formulated some personal career and lifestyle objectives, have applied some measurement targets and occasionally reflect on my progress	❑ I have formulated my personal balanced scorecard, career and personal lifestyle choices. I have defined targets, measurements and improvement actions for some objectives and occasionally update my progress.	❑ I have formulated my personal balanced scorecard (PBSC); I made career and personal lifestyle choices, set goals for continuous improvement, track my accomplishments and use the PBSC as an external reminder of my internal priorities.
1.3 Personal improvement	❑ I do not seek to improve myself on any organized basis.	❑ I seek to improve myself in some ways but have no formal way of documenting my improvements.	❑ I seek to improve myself based on my formulated personal objectives but on an ad hoc basis and have	❑ I improve myself at work and in private life based on my personal balanced scorecard and according to the Plan–Do–Act–	❑ I improve myself continuously, based on my PBSC, a living document, and the Plan–Do–Act–Challenge cycle, so I am constantly becoming

			no formal way of documenting my improvements.	Challenge cycle I am not rigorous in improving my personal effectiveness.	more conscious, authentic, creative and thus, increasing my personal effectiveness.
1.4 Personal work/life balance	❑ I do not try to balance my work and personal life. I seldom think about it.	❑ I try to keep a balance between work and personal life, but I have no process.	❑ I have taken the time to think about and develop a process to balance my work and life but do not use it rigorously	❑ I am trying to participate fully and authentically at work and in my personal life guided by my personal balanced scorecard and according to the Plan–Do–Act–Challenge cycle	❑ I consciously and continuously seek to balance my work and personal life guided by my personal balanced scorecard and the Plan–Do–Act–Challenge cycle, and I use my time more effectively.
1.5 Personal leadership	❑ I don't see myself as a leader.	❑ I sometimes consider myself a leader, but rather than worrying about others, I just want to do my job.	❑ I often lead, and others can depend on me, but I feel I could improve my personal leadership style.	❑ I see myself as a leader and attempt to manage the principles required for leadership. I am not yet effective at doing this consistently and continuously.	❑ I see myself as a leader, continuously achieve results and effectively manage the internal and external principles on which these results are based, using a leadership style founded on authenticity, intuition, openness, integrity, and trust.
1.6 Serving leadership	❑ My peers and employees see me as authoritative and directive. I do what my organization asks of me.	❑ I try to help my peers and employees.	❑ I try to put myself at the service of my peers or employees and occasionally am successful.	❑ I am learning to be there for my colleagues and employees and how to serve them such that they can achieve their objectives	❑ As a leader, I continuously put myself at the service of my colleagues and employees in a trustful manner; I spontaneously inspire, stimulate, help, and encourage them, listen to them, and appreciate their contributions.

Organizations and/or business units that achieve a certain total score and a balanced distribution of the eight dimensions qualify for the TPS Distinction or the TPS Award. Organizations and/or business units that have received a TPS Award will then be TPS certified. This TPS certification has a validity of one calendar year and can be extended based on the results of an annual audit conducted by the local TPS office and certified by an independent department within the certifying institution, TPS International Inc. in California. If you are interested in learning more about our TPS certification program, please write to us for information at:

United States

TPS International Inc.
P.O. Box 3361
Costa Mesa, CA 92628
Phone: 323-491-7424
h.rampersad@tps-international.com
info@total-performance-scorecard.com
www.total-performance-scorecard.com

TPS Great Lakes Inc.
1492 E. Drahner Road
Michigan, US 48371, USA
Phone: 416-961-2487
Fax: 416-929-2018
e.lester@tps-international.com
r.bowden@tps-international.com
www.total-performance-scorecard.com

Canada

TPS Performance Canada Ltd.
1 Balmoral Avenue, Suite 617
Toronto, Ontario
Canada M4V 3B9
Phone: (416) 972-9196
Fax:(416) 972-9261
b.angel@tps-international.com
www.total-performance-scorecard.com

Netherlands

TPS Consulting Netherlands BV
Riet Blom-Mouritsstraat 27
3066 GL Rotterdam
Netherlands
Tel: +31-653831159
info@total-performance-scorecard.com
www.Total-Performance-Scorecard.com

ABOUT THE AUTHOR

Hubert K. Rampersad, B.S., M.Sc., Ph.D., born in 1957, is an internationally respected and recognized consultant in the field of Organizational Behavior and Business Management. He is Chairman of the Board and President of TPS International Inc., California. He received his formal education in The Netherlands earning a B.S. in Mechanical Engineering, a M.Sc. in Mechanical Engineering and Robotics from Delft University of Technology, and a Ph.D. in Management from Eindhoven University of Technology. Dr. Rampersad is author of 12 books and more than 100 articles in leading international journals. His international bestseller *Total Performance Scorecard* has been translated in 22 languages. His related article was awarded with "The most outstanding paper" in the UK. His latest book *Personal Balanced Scorecard* has already been translated in 12 languages. He is a member of the Editorial Advisory Board of the journal *Training and Management Development Methods* (United Kingdom), member of the Editorial Advisory Board of the journal *Measuring Business Excellence* (United Kingdom), member of the Editorial Advisory Board of the *TQM Magazine* (United Kingdom), member of the Editorial Advisory Board of the *Journal of Knowledge Management Practice* in Canada, and editorial advisor to *Singapore Management Review*. Dr. Rampersad has conducted workshops and seminars for leading companies, such as Nokia, Philips Electronics, and

Personal Balanced Scorecard, pages 181–186

Lucent Technologies. He is also honorary professor at Ural State University in Russia.

From 1987 on he has been successful as an international management consultant guiding, coaching, and training leading organizations in the areas of his professional interest: organizational behavior, strategic management, total quality management, organizational learning, knowledge management, performance management, leadership, organizational transformation, and leading complex change. His mission statement is: *Sharing knowledge is my joy, especially if, by doing this, my work can mean something in the life of others.* The writing of this book has been a continuing learning process for him. If you would like to keep track of the latest developments in this field, please visit the website at *www.Total-Performance-Scorecard.com.* Dr. Rampersad can be reached at *h.rampersad@tps-international.com.* Total Performance Scorecard™ and Personal Balanced Scorecard™ are worldwide registered trademarks. For more information about the Total Performance Scorecard and Personal Balanced Scorecard concept, please write to:

United States

TPS International Inc.
P.O. Box 3361
Costa Mesa, CA 92628
Phone: 323-491-7424
h.rampersad@tps-international.com
info@total-performance-scorecard.com
www.total-performance-scorecard.com

TPS Great Lakes Inc.
1492 E. Drahner Road
Michigan, US 48371, USA
Phone: 416-961-2487
Fax: 416-929-2018
e.lester@tps-international.com
r.bowden@tps-international.com
www.total-performance-scorecard.com

Canada

TPS Performance Canada Ltd.
1 Balmoral Avenue, Suite 617
Toronto, Ontario
Canada M4V 3B9
Phone: (416) 972-9196
Fax:(416) 972-9261
b.angel@tps-international.com
www.total-performance-scorecard.com

Total Performance Scorecard™

TPS

Personal Balanced Scorecard™

PBSC

Netherlands

TPS Consulting Netherlands BV
Riet Blom-Mouritsstraat 27
3066 GL Rotterdam
Netherlands
Tel: +31-653831159
info@total-performance-scorecard.com
www.Total-Performance-Scorecard.com

Germany

TPS Germany GmbH
Köningsallee 60 F, 40212 Düsseldorf, Germany
Tel.: +49 211 8903 681, Fax: +49 211 8903 999
tps-germany@total-performance-scorecard.com
www.total-performance-scorecard.com

South America

TPS–PERFORMANCE DO BRASIL
Av. Brig. Faria Lima 1931, 10 andar
01451-917 - São Paulo - SP - Brasil
Tel: +55-11-3816-3144
Fax: +55-11-3819-9621
jorge@ml.com.br
www.tpsbrasil.com.br

Asia-Pacific

PT. TPS Consulting Indonesia
J.l. Melawai XII-XIII Blok N-1
Kebayoran Baru, Jakarta 12160, Indonesia
Phone: +62-21-7278-7276
Fax: +62-21-7278-7276
indra.uno@tps-indonesia.com
www.tps-indonesia.com

We are devoted to helping individuals and organizations become more successful. We provide integrated and sustainable professional services (consulting and training) based on the proven Total Performance Scorecard and Personal Balanced Scorecard principles. The results are individual and organizational effectiveness and a related unique competitive advantage. Call or write us for information on our international office closest to you, or for a free catalog of TPS & PBSC products and programs.

JEANNETTE LEE (Author of the Foreword)

Jeannette Lee is a business owner, entrepreneur, and founder of the award-winning information technology company Sytel, Inc. She earned the national Entrepreneurial Excellence Award from *Working Woman* magazine in 2000. She served as President and CEO of Sytel from inception in 1987 to 2005, the year in which Sytel was acquired by Techteam Global Inc.

She graduated with a degree in economics with honors from The George Washington University in Washington, D.C. in 1983, and received executive education from Dartmouth and completed a YPO/MIT Presidents' Seminar on eBusiness at MIT. She is the founder of Sytel, an information technology infrastructure service provider which specializes in enterprise network integration, network management, and IT helpdesk, application integration, and enterprise network and system security. Sytel has received numerous other awards and recognitions for high-quality performance and fast growth. Sytel has been named one of the 500 fastest growing companies in America by *Inc.* magazine (1994, 1996, 1997, 1998, and 1999) and among the fastest growing U.S. technology firms listed by Deloitt & Touche (1995–1998).

As a 5-time *Inc. 500* winner in 1999, Sytel was one of four companies in the U.S. inducted into *Inc.*'s Hall of Fame, an honor shared by Microsoft, Domino's Pizza, E*Trade, and others. Lee has been directly involved in Sytel since its inception. As the company grew, she continued to actively lead the company's activities. Teamwork, inner strength, vision, strong culture and especially capacity of adaptation seem to be the pillars for the success of Sytel and its founder. "The company has already gone through three big changes, and I have been constantly transforming myself over the past 20 years," Lee stated to *The Washington Post* in 2001. "I've transformed myself more than I ever could have imagined was possible."

Lee has been recognized nationally and locally as a business leader in the Montgomery County community. In 1998 Lee was selected as the Executive of the Year, by the High Tech Council of Maryland. That same year, she was also given the 1998 Entrepreneurial Award by the Dialogue on Diversity and named among the top entrepreneurs in the country by Success magazine. In 2000, Lee won a national Entrepreneurial Excellence Award in the field of Innovative Business Strategies category from the Working Woman magazine. In 2001, Lee was listed as the *Washingtonian* magazine's "100 Most Powerful Women in Washington." This list consists of thirteen categories, covering subjects including Religion, Health Care, Education, Legal Authorities, and National and Local powers. Lee was named for her success in the Business category, and shares this honor with First Lady Laura Bush, Lynne Cheney, Sandra Day O'Connor and Senator Hillary Clinton. Lee was also recognized as the annual honoree by the Boy Scouts of America, Potomac Maryland chapter.

In addition, Lee belongs to several community and business organizations. She served as the founding member on the Governor-appointed Board of the Maryland Technology Development Corporation (Tedco); served on the Board of Trustees of The George Mason University Foundation; and served on the Board of Directors of the High Tech Council of Maryland. She was also member of the Board of Visitors of the Maryland School of Public Affairs/University of Maryland, and of the Board of Directors for the Greater Washington Board of Trade, the most active business organization for the entire region.

Lee served as a Washington Metro chapter officer of the Young Presidents' Organization, an exclusive organization of 8,500 presidents and CEOs worldwide; and also served as Chairwoman of Montgomery United Way (2000–2001).

Lee spoke on business management topics at an annual Young Entrepreneurs' Organization conference in Toronto, Canada, as Solomon Smith Barney-sponsored and selected presenter; spoke at Women in MBA at Wharton, MIT Forum, and at various industry conferences; Lee has been a guest lecturer at Georgetown MBA School for the past several years.

REFERENCES AND RECOMMENDED READING

Accenture, *The Point: The Difference Makers; How Workforces Can Propel Companies from Mediocrity to High Performance? www.accenture.com*

Agor, W., *Management by Consciousness* (edited by G.P. Gupta), Sri Aurobindo Institute of Research in Social Sciences, Pondicherry, India, 1998.

Angel, R. and H.K. Rampersad, *Do Balanced Scorecards Add Up?*, Toronto: CA Magazine Performance, 2005.

Bowden, R.M., *Transforming Stress into Productivity*, Michigan: Transformation Inc. 2006

Business for Social Responsibility (BSR), *http://www.bsr.org/*, US, 2005.

Chatterejee, D., *Light the Fire in Your Heart*. New Delhi: Full Circle Publishing, 2002.

Chatterejee, D., *Leading Consciously*. Boston: Butterworth-Heinemann, 1998.

Chopra Deepak, *The Seven Spiritual Laws of Success*, Amber-Allen Publishing, San Francisco, 1995.

Covey, S.R., *The Seven Habits of Highly Effective People*, Simon & Schuster, New York, 1993.

Covey, S.R., *The 8th Habit*, Simon & Schuster, New York, 2004.

Csikszentmihalyi, Mihaly, *Flow: The Psychology of Optimal Experience*, HarperCollins Publishers, New York, 1990.

Deming, W.E., *Out of the Crisis*, Cambridge: Massachusetts Institute of Technology, 1985.

Evans, R., and P. Russell, *De Creatieve Manager*, Cothen, Utrecht: Servire, 1991.

Grimm, G., *Buddhist Wisdom: The Mystery of the Self*, Motilal Banarsidas Publishers Pvt. Ltd., Delhi, 1999.

Hamel, G., and C.K. Prahalad, *Competing for the Future: Breakthrough Strategies for Seizing Control of your Industry and Creating Markets of Tomorrow*, Boston: Harvard Business School Press, 1994.

Handy, C., *Understanding Voluntary Organizations*, Hammersworth, UK: Penguin Books, 1988.

Personal Balanced Scorecard, pages 187–189

Jacobs, G., *Management by Consciousness* (edited by G.P. Gupta), Sri Aurobindo Institute of Research in Social Sciences, Pondicherry, India, 1998.

Kaplan, R.S. and D.P. Norton, *The Strategy-focused Organization: how balanced scorecard companies thrive in the new business environment,* Harvard Business School Press, Boston, 2000.

Kaplan, R.S. and D.P. Norton, *Strategy Maps: Converting Intangible Assets into Tangible Outcomes,* Harvard Business School Press, Boston, 2003.

Kolb, D.A., *Experiential Learning,* Englewood Cliffs, NJ: Prentice-Hall, 1984.

Kouzes, J.M., and B.Z. Posner, *Een hart onder de riem: hoe kan ik anderen erkenning geven en belonen?* Schiedam, Schiedam: Scriptum Management, 1999.

Krueger Jerry and Emily Killham. At Work, Feeling Good Matters, New York: Gallup Management Journal,

December 08, 2005.

Kovach, K.A. "What Motivates Employees? Workers and Supervisors Give Different Answers", *Business Horizons* 30 (1987), pp. 59–60.

Leifer, R., *The Happiness Project,* New York: Snow Lion Publications, 1997.

Lester, E., *KAM II Principles of Human Development,* Walden University, 2006

Leonard, D., *Wellsprings of Knowledge: Building and Sustaining the Source of Innovation,* Boston: Harvard Business School Press, 1998.

McCraty, R., The Scientific Role of the Heart in Learning and Performance, *HeartMath Research Center, Institute of HeartMath, Publication No. 02-030, Boulder Creek, CA, 2002.*

Maslow, A.H., *Motivation and Personality,* New York: Harper & Row, 1970.

Miller, D.S., S.E. Catt, and J.R. Carlson, *Fundamentals of Management: A Framework for Excellence.* Minneapolis, MN: West Publishing Company, 1996.

Miller, W.C., and P. Pruzan, *Spiritual-based Leadership: A Matter of Faith and Confidence,* Puttaparthi: Sri Sathya Sai Institute of Higher Learning, 2003.

Rampersad, H.K., *Total Performance Scorecard; Redefining Management to Achieve Performance with Integrity,* Butterworth-Heinemann Business Books, Elsevier Science, Massachusetts, 2003.

Rampersad, H.K., *Managing Total Quality; Enhancing Personal and Company Value,* Tata McGraw-Hill, New Delhi, 2005.

Rampersad, H.K., *Personal Balanced Scorecard, Tata McGraw-Hill,* New Delhi, *2005.*

Rampersad, H.K., and Kari Tuominen, *Total Performance Scorecard; Selfassessment Workbook,* Tata McGraw-Hill, New Delhi, 2006.

Schein, E.H., *Organizational Culture and Leadership: A Dynamic View.* San Francisco: Jossey-Bass, 1992.

Senge, P.M., *The Fifth Discipline: The Art and Practice of the Learning Organization.* New York: Doubleday, 1990.

Sharma, R.S., *The Top 200 Secrets of Success and the Pillars of Self-Mastery, http://www.robinsharma.com*

Sri Sri Ravi Shankar, *Wisdom for the New Millennium,* Art of Living Foundation, Chicago, 1999.

Thompson, A.A., and A.J. Strickland, *Strategic Management: Concepts and Cases,* Boston: McGraw-Hill, 2002.

Wanrooy, M.J., *Leidinggeven Tussen Professionals,* Scriptum Management, Schiedam, 2001.

Ulrich, D., and D. Lake, *Organizational Capability: Competing from the Inside Out*, New York: John Wiley & Sons, 1990.

Wise, A., *The High Performance Mind—Mastering Brainwaves for Insight, Healing, and Creativity*, Tarcher Putnam, 1995.

Yesudian, S., *Sta op en wees vrij; gedachten en gesprekken over yoga*, Ankh-Hermes b.v., Deventer, 1991.

INDEX

Personal Balanced Scorecard, pages 191–195

Q

R

Printed in the United States
86187LV00003B/154/A

9 781593 115319